FREEDOM IS YOUR
HUMAN RIGHT!

Also by Dianna L. Grayer, M.F.T.
Journaling: Getting to Know Yourself

FREEDOM IS YOUR HUMAN RIGHT!

ACCEPTING AND HONORING YOURSELF

by

DIANNA L. GRAYER, M.F.T.

I'm Special Publications
✳❖✳❖✳❖
Petaluma, California

Freedom Is Your Human Right!:
Accepting and Honoring Yourself
by Dianna L. Grayer, M.F.T.

Book Editing and Layout by Netty Kahan
Book Cover Design by Kevin Gilfether
Photograph by Sheridan L. Gold

Publisher's Cataloging-in-Publication
(Provided by Quality Books, Inc.)

Grayer, Dianna L.
   Freedom is your human right! : accepting and honoring yourself / by Dianna L. Grayer--1st ed.
   p. cm.
   Includes index.
   ISBN 0-9660507-1-1

   1. Self-esteem. 2. Lesbian--Psychology. 3. Gays--Psychology. 4. Bisexuals--Psychology. 5. Transsexuals --Psychology. I. Title.

BF697.5.S46G73 2003   305.9'0664
                        QB133-1090

Published by I'm Special Publications
P.O. Box 452, Petaluma, CA 94953
707-793-9840 Office and Fax

Printed in the United States of America

This book is dedicated to LGBTs
Because you are worthy human beings
Who deserve to be acknowledged, counted, and free

CONTENTS

Foreward and Forward! x

Preface xii
Where did this book come from and what's it about? xii
How to use this book xiii

Acknowledgements xvi
I Have a Dream xvii

Introduction: Motivation 1
Why Is It That My Heart Continuously Hurts? 4
Why Would I? 5
God Bless America 7
Freedom Is Your Human Right 9

Freedom Is a Sacrifice 11
We Can't Be Satisfied 18
We Must Stand Strong 22
The Human Race 24
Don't Tell Me What to Do 26

Get Mad 27

Get Mad Process 32

I Am the Wind 34
Rejection 37
Displaced Attention 39
All of Me 40

Healing Your Emotional Wounds 41

Taking the Journey 50
God I Know You Accept Me 52
Slow Down 54
Don't Quit—Don't Give Up 56

Soul-Searching 57

Other Questions to Explore 76
I Will Not Stop My Life 78

Removing the Chains of Bondage 79

Look at Me 89
FYI—To the President and His Cabinet 91
I Am Free 92

Who Am I, Really? 93

Challenge I 97

Stand Up and Be Counted 99

The Light 101

What Do I Have to Do?   102

Challenge II   105
   I Pledge Allegiance to Myself   107

Columns   109
   Creating Family   109
   In Honor of Our Friend   111
   Beating Fear   112
   How Can We Count Ourselves If We Don't Know
      Who We Are?   114
   You Are Your Best Resource   115
   Seeing Our Parents, Seeing Ourselves   117
   True Freedom   119
   Get Out of Your Comfort Zone   120
   Time Is Flying   122
   Is Rejection Always a Bad Thing?   123
   Communicating Is Like Dancing   125
   Find Your Balance   126
   Have a Heart   128
   Receiving Is Part of Self-Care   129
   Learning the Couple Dance   130
   Family — At What Price?   132

Index   134

Foreword and Forward!

Dianna Grayer's book *Freedom Is Your Human Right* is a book of evolution. Stemming from Dianna's well-developed thoughts and processes, the form of the book itself evolves through different stages; and the reader progresses as they read and work through the challenges presented. Dianna Grayer poses ideas that are both provocative and so healthy that as I read them I thought, "Of course. Why haven't I thought that before?" Her words—reaped from the hard work she has done on herself and the growth she has helped her clients through—first move from righteous indignation to a vital sense of entitlement and constructive, empowering anger. While so many strong speakers and thinkers would stop there, Dianna makes clear that the essential partner to these feelings is self-understanding through soul-searching as well as learning to remove inner bonds and release the pains from the past. Readers are led to recognize the messages from others that they have internalized and the emotional wounds that have festered within them. As readers look within and give themselves space for reflection, Dianna gives them tools to help process their emerging feelings until they are truly thriving people.

As a passionate, dedicated encourager and challenger—challenging LGBTs to get angry, to love themselves, and to do their emotional work—Dianna teaches how to move along these stepping-stones. She explains some of the dynamics of psychological pain and defenses, so people can understand themselves better. In reading this book, you, too, will probably find yourself pushed up against some of your personal emotional barriers: Be patient and give yourself a chance; most likely you will move through the blocks and have a fuller life as the reward. Finally, this book is a book of release—release from bondage and release of your internalized pain, so you can make room for joy and vitality.

Freedom Is Your Human Right! is multifaceted: It provides thoughts that push the readers' buttons and illuminates them. And it's a politically stimulating book. Dianna's thoughts expand the reader to think about what America's fight to preserve freedom is all about and joggles them to recognize the power that could come from LGBTs insisting on their entitlement to be acknowledged as humans with the right to freedom.

Dianna earns the right to write on the topic because she lives what she espouses: In person, her intermingled strength and compassion are evident. Her self-confidence, as well as her gentle understanding of others and her sense of fun, inspire and wake up those around. In working with her and getting to know her, I have felt motivated by her tremendous energy, creativity, and multifaceted talents. So, be aware that as you read and work with this book, you might feel irritable and pushed against the wall. But it's good stuff. Dianna has her heart in the right place and has witnessed these processes work with herself and her clients.

—Netty Kahan, Editor
Novato, California

Preface

Where Did this Book Come From and What's It About?

I always knew that I would write books focused on helping people be the best they can be. I wanted to help people learn to be okay with who they are and teach them that they have the power within to change what they don't like in themselves and their lives. I always sought ways to heal people, and becoming a therapist was an important avenue toward my goal: It allowed me intimate contact with clients. However, I still yearned to reach more people.

Then, I had an opportunity to reach a larger number of people when I met Kay Mehl Miller, a journalist who writes a column for a local newspaper, *We the People.* The newspaper, which serves the gay community, was looking for lesbian writers; so Kay suggested I give them a call. This was perfect for me because the LGBT (Lesbian, Gay, Bisexual & Transgender) community has always been one of several focal points of my energy and passion. My articles all focus on building up individuals and teaching them to love themselves—that they matter and are a priority.

Knowing that people suffer on a daily basis, I wanted to find more ways to help. I began writing books and leading workshops to help others fully claim their lives.

Then this book surfaced when the 9/11/01 World Trade Center tragedy shook up nearly everyone in America, in many different ways. My thoughts and passions were deeply affected by attitudes that came out in reference to the military's "Don't ask, Don't tell" policy toward LGBTs: When I heard a government official state that the country could overlook that now while they go off to war, I was infuriated by the audacity to accept us at their convenience, and I had to write this book to speak out. I began to think about the irony of America going to war to preserve freedom in the world without honoring freedom here at home.

)(❖)(

It is with great pleasure that I share with you a collection of writings from deep in my heart and soul that continue to inspire me every day. Each piece has come as a result of being moved, stirred up, or enlightened in my day-to-day life experiences on my path toward healing. My journey has been incredible, and even though it's been full of emotional pain, inner conflict, and personal struggles, it has been very satisfying and rewarding to my soul and inner spirit.

I believe that where there is pain, there can be growth.

I'm hoping that what you will experience in the following pages will be an opening that will lead and guide you to enormous growth and healing. Such work is needed for one to connect to their soul. Connecting to your soul will connect you to your life. Valuing your life will naturally assist you in living your life to its fullest.

Pay attention to what your inner voice is saying as you go on your journey. You will have times of creative unfolding when your own words will flow from within like a steady stream. Words that symbolize compassion, passion, and a deeper meaning and value for yourself will want to surface. Open up to free expression. Don't fight the feelings—let them out. Let your voice, heart, and soul speak and discover the answers you have been wanting. Make time to write and express what's inside of you. Unleash yourself!

If you are interested and want to tap into the real you—deep in your soul—then you must begin to spend time alone, special time with just yourself so you can listen to your spirit. For your life to improve, you must be able to hear the answers to your questions. So, let your soul speak to you and give you the guidance you need to change and enhance your life. Your answers are within yourself. You just need to be quiet enough to hear what is being said.

How to Use this Book
Within the covers of this book, you will find the means to discover and relate to more of what is within yourself. These pages contain a medley of challenging thoughts and growth exercises for your empowerment and self-discovery; the prose is intermingled with poems born from my self-

expression and self-discovery. Also included at the end of the book are newspaper columns I co-wrote for *We the People.*

This book was set up to help you explore yourself: to help you learn how you value yourself and your freedom. You'll find here questions to help you learn what's inside of you and what you stand for. You will discover and release your rage, which will guide you and motivate you to act. Your purpose and worth will become clear, and you will realize that you, too, deserve to be free. This is your work: You owe it to yourself and your life.

Answer the questions as fully and thoroughly as possible. Don't hold back. Make time to reflect on your life. This is your process, for your eyes only. If you haven't been honest with yourself before, then it's time you are. You have tried to hide, but we all know you haven't been successful—inevitably, your dishonesty shows itself somewhere, and you don't feel good about it. Your journey—if you choose to accept the challenge—will help you discover that what is really important is yourself. You have to trust and believe in yourself and know you are worth your time and energy.

Also included in this book are poems and prose to motivate and support you. I believe in you and the human spirit. Growth and self-healing are processes that can't be rushed, which makes this a book to work with over several sessions. It's not the kind of book you can take in at one sitting. Although you are likely to experience some of your resistance as you work with the exercises and read thoughts—as they push you up against some of your "internal walls"—if you are patient with yourself and come back to working with *Freedom Is Your Human Right!* you will reap the treasures of your breakthroughs and liberation.

I recommend that you read the prose in the book in sequence, because it is, in part, the building of an argument or case. The poems interspersed throughout the book can give a break (a "minivacation") from some of the effort of working on yourself. The poems might give expression to some of the feelings evoked in you from the writings and exercises. Read the poems as is your pleasure.

)(❖)(

I want to wake up the LGBTs all over the world, especially right here at home in America, and I'm hoping that after the terrorist attacks they want to be awakened. I know my words of wisdom, strength, and belief in the human spirit are ready to be shared. The terrorist attacks served as the catalyst to get me started on the work I was destined to do. I need to teach LGBTs new ways of loving and accepting themselves and of thinking about themselves. I need to encourage and support all LGBTs to find their inner strength and fight for their freedom.

I wish you well on your journey to that "place" where you believe, know, and act as though freedom is your human right. May all your dreams come true and the rest of your life be filled with all that you truly are.

Cooboday,
Dianna

Cooboday (pronounced "Coo-bah'-day") is a word I've created to express "Grant strength, courage, and guidance." It's derived from *coup*, meaning "take over," and *body*.

Acknowledgments

I thank God for giving me strength, courage, and the wisdom to believe in myself and to always know that I am a valued human being—deserving of respect and freedom. I thank the Great Spirit for guidance and for my ability to heal others. I am grateful for God being there through my difficult, stressful, and painful times. Throughout many years of not having a human ear to listen to my cries, I could always depend on God being there to hear my tears, fears, happiness, dreams, thoughts, and all my feelings. Because of the Great Spirit, I am here today doing the work I am destined to do, which is to move people toward inner peace and freedom. God, thank you for your blessings and for showing me the light.

I HAVE A DREAM

I have a dream that one day
I will not be judged by my sexual orientation,
but by who I am.
I have a dream

I have a dream that one day
I will be able to walk down the street arm and arm
with my partner and rejoice.
I have a dream

I have a dream that one day
I will live in a society where there is love and compassion for all people,
not hate and violence.
I have a dream

I have a dream that one day
An innocent precious beautiful child, who might feel different than you,
will feel safe to say so.
I have a dream

I have a dream that one day
When that child shares with you, you will hold, comfort, protect, love,
and respect that child.
I have a dream

I have a dream that one day
Business women and men, politicians, religious groups,
people in power, leaders, and educators of all cultures,
will come to support, celebrate, honor and respect diversity,
not destroy it.
I have a dream

I have a dream that one day
All God's children, including gays, lesbians, bisexuals, transgenders
and all the other people who are different, and feel different,
will be accepted as worthy people,
because we are.
I have a dream

I have a dream that one day
I am seen for myself, my good deeds, my compassion for life,
my contributions, how I live my life,
because ...
I am somebody. Yes I am.
I have a dream

I have a dream—
women and men, boys and girls—
Yes, I have a dream, an important dream.
It's a dream of acceptance and freedom.
I have a dream

By Dianna L. Grayer
11/23/97

INSPIRED BY DR. MARTIN LUTHER KING JR.

INTRODUCTION: MOTIVATION

When the 9/11/01 World Trade Center tragedy shocked America and the world, I got moving on this book. The moment that propelled me in front of my computer was when a government official stated to the country that the military was going to overlook the "Don't ask, Don't tell" policy at this time. I became livid. Feelings were stirred up so intensely inside my heart, and my mind was churning incredibly fast. I needed to do something. I wanted to speak out and have everyone hear what I had to say.

During this crisis everything we heard was about *freedom* and about all Americans standing together. I wanted to join forces and stand together with my LGBT sisters and brothers. All that talk around freedom stimulated me because I know that within America, although we say we're a free country, many Americans *aren't free.*

I was blown away by what happened with the terrorist attacks; I thought about the amount of evil that's within a person to make them do such an unthinkable act upon human lives. However, the issue that compelled me to write is how people are being treated right here in America. I know what's really happening around me. I know what *I've* experienced, and I have heard many disturbing experiences from others and the media.

)(❖)(

I have seen injustice, discrimination, and pain experienced by LGBTs and all races of people: Blacks, Whites, Latinos, Native Americans, Asians, and Pacific Islanders. The reality is that people have been degraded, abused, unaccepted, disrespected, and teased for so long that they have to struggle to love and honor themselves. Their pain has motivated me—to help rid them of such unnecessary baggage.

I believe human nature is good and that it just needs to be tended to. In the way that a neglected garden can go into disarray, so the unnurtured person becomes unable to express his or her beauty and vitality. My role is to teach people, especially LGBTs, how to take care of

1

themselves and to help them learn new skills to live a healthier, more meaningful, and happier life. My goal also is to help them understand how they continue a negative cycle by not fighting back for their lives. With my God-given strength and wisdom, I aim to guide them through, onto their paths to inner peace and freedom.

Yes, you are a priority
and you owe it to yourself to be free.

I believe no matter how much pain you're in and how much abuse you have suffered, you can do more than just survive—you can truly be alive. You can live in your body and learn to protect yourself. You can learn to never let another person hurt you. You can learn to respect yourself and refuse to tolerate disrespect from others. You can learn to overcome your fears, as you grow to love, accept, and believe in yourself. You can learn to live free and be happy. All this can be, but it begins with you—from within.

I can't tolerate unfairness. Therefore, I made the decision to take a stand by writing this book: to open the eyes of LGBTs and others who choose to read my words. I hope you, the reader, will join in the fight for respect, acknowledgment, acceptance, protection, and freedom for all.

People of color still struggle daily to be free, while affirmative action has been revoked. Where are the equality, fairness, and freedom in this? LGBTs find themselves in the same situation: struggling for freedom. LGBTs are not free. Look at the numbers of LGBTs who are in, rather than out, of the closet. This is because many heterosexuals, especially white men in power and many in religious groups, believe being LGBT is an abomination, a sin. This attitude hinders LGBTs from accepting and honoring themselves. I am not an abomination and neither are you. And here we are, at war with Afghanistan and talking about going to war with Iraq to fight for our freedom—*whose* freedom?

As the days went by, America was grieving and many were frightened for what might be in our future. My attention was focused on the statement made to the LGBTs serving our country and on how they and civilian LGBTs were responding. I lingered in disbelief that anyone would make a statement so insensitive—especially during a time of enormous suffering, chaos, and devastation. How disrespectful!

Who is this running our country, anyway? If the government expects respect, then they should give it. This was definitely another slap in the face. The first slap was not to accept (open) gays and lesbians in the military. And then now in effect to say, "It's okay, just during wartime." Here again was the message to the LGBT community that we're not okay and that we can be chewed up and spit out when we're no longer needed. I felt such urgency, which motivated me to write this book.

LGBTs all over the world, especially right here at home in America, need to be awakened. We need to learn how to love and accept who we are—to know that, just like heterosexuals, we deserve to be free and respected and are entitled to all the privileges and benefits available to heterosexuals. It is time to make our move to change the thinking and laws of America to protect *all* its people. It's our time to stand up and be counted.

If the government expects respect, then they should give it . . . LGBTs deserve to be free and respected and are entitled to all the privileges and benefits available to heterosexuals . . . It is time to make our move to change the thinking and laws of America to protect all its people. It's our time to stand up and be counted.

WHY IS IT THAT MY HEART CONTINUOUSLY HURTS?

Why is it that my heart continuously hurts?
Are you watching what I'm watching?
Are you seeing what I'm seeing?
Are you hearing what I'm hearing?

I sense an enormous need for fairness,
justice, and equality.
I sense an enormous need for freedom.
I sense an enormous need to make
life better for all.

When I look in the mirror I see a Black face.
Where is my representation in the media?
When I look in the mirror I see a lesbian.
Where is my representation in the media?
From one oppression to the next,

My reflection is not accepted.
What will it be next,
My shape?
My size?
My hairstyle?
What part of me or you will be unacceptable next?

Why is it that my heart continuously hurts?
Are you watching what I'm watching?
Are you seeing what I'm seeing?
Are you hearing what I'm hearing?

By Dianna L. Grayer
1/11/2000

WHY WOULD I?

My name is Dianna.
I am somebody.
All that I do.
All that I am.
Is me!
I am proud of who I am.
I am Black.
I am Lesbian.
I am tall.
I am strong.
I am a healer.
I am talented.
I am confident.
I am smart.
I am kind.
I am happy.
I am blessed.
I am me.

So, why would I want to change who I am?
Why would I want to change myself when I'm happy with myself?
Why would I want to deny the essence of who I am?
Why would I?
Why would I reject myself
because you and others like you
can't—or won't—accept a certain part of me?
Why would I tear myself down and think ill of myself
because of you and your feelings of me?
Why would I give up my freedom?
My human right.

Your hatred.
Your ignorance.
Your intolerance.
Your lack of acceptance.
Your lack of understanding.

Your inability to embrace diversity.
Your choice to be closed minded.
All of this. It's about you.
Not me!

So, I say again.
Why would I?
Why would I hurt me when I love me?
All of me!

By: Dianna L. Grayer
9/16/01

GOD BLESS AMERICA (SONG)

God Bless America
To do the right thing
Take your people
All your people
Make them all proud enough that they'll sing
About the freedom
For all colors
all religions
Equality
God Bless America
You can succeed
Justice for everyone
We have the need

God Bless America
Serve all who reside
Stand beside them
And love them
So that they can feel a part and not hide
Yes the dark ones
And the light ones
And the gay ones,
Trans Bi too
Let's choose equality
Not just for the few
Cherish our country land
For me and you

God Bless America
This is our home
We have this moment
To cherish
All that we are together and alone

Work for justice
and acceptance
For equality
and for peace
We are America
This is our dream
We have the ability
To do
the right
thing

By Sheridan L. Gold
Inspired by a poem by Dianna L. Grayer
9/16/01

FREEDOM IS YOUR HUMAN RIGHT

Freedom is your human right.
Freedom is my human right.
Freedom is our human right.
You must agree because
there's no room to disagree.

We must strive to be free.
Each and every one of us.
Because there's no other way for it to be.
Push ahead and don't be swayed.
We're all joining hands and help is on the way.

Freedom is for you and for me.
It doesn't matter the color of your skin.
Your sexual orientation.
Your religion.
Your size or shape.
It's our human right.

Freedom is acceptance of all our differences.
Freedom is respecting our experiences.
Freedom is embracing the life of each one of us.
Freedom is living life to its fullest.

Remove your chains.
Remove your bondage.
Remove your fear.
Rip them off and set yourself free.
Find your worth and you'll be free.
Fight for your human right.
Fight for your right to be free.

Pay attention to the immigrants.
And learn their ways.
They know what it takes to be free.
They know the value of being free,
Risky business I should say.

Stand up and be proud.
Stand up and be counted.
Stand up and fight for your right.
Stand up and let freedom reign.
Stand up and accept your human right.

Freedom is your human right.
Freedom is my human right.
Freedom is our human right.
You must agree because
there's no room to disagree.

By Dianna L. Grayer
11/1/01

FREEDOM IS A SACRIFICE

History has shown all of us from oppressed groups that freedom is not a given: If you want it, you must pay a huge price as you fight for it.

Odd as it may sound,
one has to fight to be free here in America.

Unfortunately, this is the way it is and the way it has always been. Martin Luther King Jr. made a major impact for civil rights, and he was shot down. He sacrificed not only for himself, but also for a race of people. People before him and after him have died—and many others will continue to die—as they made the sacrifice of fighting for freedom. Here we are in 2002 and again we're at war for freedom. Let's face it, fighting for freedom is a risk and a sacrifice. It can cost you your life. Some will weather the storm, and some won't. Take a moment and ask yourself these questions: Why is the price for freedom so high? Why can't people just accept differences and let people be who they are?

You would think that in going to war to fight for freedom—this battle in which the fighters include people from diverse backgrounds— everyone would be able to reap the benefits, especially if we would win the war. It makes sense to feel that all Americans are entitled to and should be able to experience freedom, that freedom would reign over our country and all the people would be happy. However, for some ungodly reason, this is not the American way. It seems the American way is to have a foot pressing on another's throat, suffocating her or him.

You would think that in going to war to fight for freedom—this battle in which the fighters include people from all diverse backgrounds—everyone would be able to reap the benefits, especially if we would win the war.

White America, especially most heterosexual men, understand the value of freedom and make sure it is secure for them and their families. However their understanding and sensitivity doesn't sustain itself enough to share that freedom and sense of security with the rest of us. We get the garbage. We don't matter. Our throats are where they're resting their feet. They're suffocating us, and we're letting them do it. Each and every one of us who has chosen to hide and not be counted perpetuates the situation. We must remove them from our throats to catch our breath.

If you want to be free, you must make the decision to fight, to make the sacrifice. It's dangerous and hard work, and it will test your strength and courage.

You have to remove your oppressor's feet off your throat so you can breathe and live. You have to tell yourself you want to do more than live, you want to live **free***.*

You have to be okay with being uncomfortable while knowing that—like with any other challenge or experience you're unfamiliar with—you will learn to be comfortable. This is your life. You can only win by doing your part in fighting for your life. By doing nothing, you have already lost. You will die trying or die lying. It's your choice.

These choices are difficult for many people. Everyone wants to win, but unfortunately life doesn't work that way. All races, religions, and sexual orientations are sacrificing and dying right now as they fight for your freedom. Many people of color have died fighting for their freedom because of the color of their skin. Many LGBTs have died also. Matthew Sheppard, for example, was brutally murdered because of his sexual orientation. He was only trying to live a free life. If someone must die, let it be for a worthy cause, your freedom.

We've all heard it said that life is the survival of the fittest. What does this really mean as it relates to humans? Does it mean that the one in the best shape or the one who is smartest will survive the longest? Or does it mean the one with the best weapons will win the war? Many different interpretations or conclusions can be drawn from this quote. It really doesn't matter how smart or strong you are. What matters is where your rage is. We know that when a person's adrenaline kicks in there is no limit to his or her strength.

$$)(\diamond)($$

We all need to start raging—not in a violent way, but with powerful hearts that are determined to make changes. We need our adrenaline to wake us up. This means we need to stop slouching and start standing strong. I believe if we all rage together and let our oppressors see our strength in numbers, we all can be free people.

Imagine this:

What if all the American soldiers who are members of oppressed groups— people of color, gays, lesbians, women, Jews, and atheists—refused to go to war? This would have a huge impact on the number of military personnel and would make a profound and extremely visual statement for the American people. People could see the strength that lies in diversity. To take it further, what if the soldiers would make a deal agreeing to return to the war if their freedom was granted to them after the war? This makes especially good sense because this is the very reason that is stated for why we are fighting a war in the first place.

$$)(\diamond)($$

What is horrifying is that oppressed people, especially LGBTs, don't do this. It saddens me to know that many LGBTs tolerate the way they are treated. We allow what is happening to our people in America to keep happening. We allow ourselves to be treated unfairly and disrespectfully. Our sisters and brothers and other members of oppressed groups have died at home and abroad—for what and for whom? What were they fighting for? And if they were abroad and survived, they returned home to a country that didn't embrace them, but rather shamed and blamed them. For them, there was no freedom to be won from the beginning.

They were brainwashed as are the majority of us. LGBTs allow themselves to stay in a one-down position. What about equality? Where is your fight to be free? You cannot let homophobia keep you down, afraid, imprisoned, and unable to live a free life. Don't let the homophobics' issue become yours. Give it back to them. It's their problem.

You must find within yourself the energy and strength equal to that same energy and strength that you use to keep yourself in the closet, and use it to set yourself free.

Demand your freedom—which is your human right. Stand up for yourself and for what is right.

Dying is frightening to most people, so to avoid risk, they avoid living their lives to the fullest. I believe if I'm going to fight in a war, the cause must be great. Our freedom is a great cause. But if we're not going to be granted our freedom, then our appropriate fight is not in standing with our country, but in challenging and fighting our country to honor and accept all its people. We have only one choice: We shall stand united or we shall fall divided. Right now, we're falling. We are being killed, and we're killing ourselves by suffocating in our closets. We all are going to die at some point in our lives, so don't let dying stop you from fighting for your human right, your freedom.

Some people will die sooner and others later. Some will die from an illness and others due to an accident. Some from hate crimes. Some because they were in the wrong place at the wrong time. Some because they were involved in things they shouldn't have been. Some from acts of nature, and some from war. We don't know when or how it will happen. It is said that whenever we die it is the way it was planned.

We don't have time to waste. How many people who died in the World Trade Center (WTC) would have done things differently or changed some part of the way they were living their lives if they knew they were going to die on 9/11? Don't let your life go unfinished if you can help it. We've wasted too much time living bound in fear. Don't waste any more time being passive, waiting for your time to die. Which is worse, being killed by a hate crime or fighting someone else's war? Exactly—they're both disgusting and neither is a welcome fate. When we settle, we lose. We need to refocus and know our priorities. We need to fight our own war.

This is your wake up call. Can you hear it? What's important now is for you to wake up and see the light: Your life! It's about believing in yourself and fighting for your life. It's time for us to live our lives freely—then, when we die, we will die fulfilled and say to ourselves, it was all worth it.

No longer is it acceptable to settle for the mere portions of freedoms that America has allowed us. We have got to know and believe that we, too, deserve what others get. We must be the squeaky wheel and let ourselves be seen and heard. People must know we exist with a soul, heart, and spirit, and that we have value and worth. They must realize we're not empty shells absent of feelings: We feel, we hear, we see—and we also can fight.

We must work hard as the immigrants do. They fight and risk everything to come to the "land of the free." They would rather die trying—which many of them have—and experience freedom, than settle to dying poor, unhappy, oppressed, and unfree. You've heard the stories: Nothing is too hard for an immigrant if his or her goal is to get to America. The borders will never stop them from coming to the land of the presumed free. They epitomize what it means "to have heart." They are moved by an urgency and a knowing. We need to find that same urgency and tenacity to risk everything for freedom. We must give America back its chains and shackles, and live free.

Rosa Parks comes to mind, too. Imagine the commitment she had made to herself before she refused to give up her seat on the bus in Montgomery, Alabama. She was a woman on a mission, and she had had enough—alone she defied a law that was unjust toward Black people. Her arrest for refusing to move from her seat sparked a boycott. And, with Martin Luther King Jr.'s leadership as well as the courage of the many Blacks who joined the movement and refused to use the bus system, eventually the law changed. This outcome was huge. It shows that *one person* can make an impact toward social change—Rosa Parks led a change that benefited a race of people: Blacks, just like Whites, were finally able to sit anywhere they chose on the bus.

Rosa valued herself, so much that she risked her life for her self-worth. She did this during the time when Blacks had no rights and were being abused, battered, and lynched for the smallest infraction. Her actions clearly displayed that she wanted and deserved to have the rights, respect, and freedom that the White people had, and she knew she deserved to be treated with respect and decency. She knew her freedom was worth fighting for. Freedom *can* be won. In Rosa Parks's case it happened by her stepping forth and other sisters and brothers supporting her and uniting in the fight. She made a huge sacrifice, and today she is still here sharing her strength and courage with us all.

So I challenge you to begin doing your work and fighting for your freedom. You might be thinking, "How?" If you're impatient, that's good— that means you're with me, you're paying attention. Just keep reading, and you will know exactly what you must do. You won't have to do the treacherous things the immigrants have done, but you will have to discomfort yourself and take some risks similar to those Rosa Parks took. You have to confront someone, some group, or a law. Put out energy toward becoming a free person. We have to show ourselves in numbers. We need everyone to join in if our goal is to be a free people. This is why we must all do our part.

Remember, the immigrants didn't just one day up and leave their countries. And the bus boycott didn't just happen. Such things take time and planning. It is a process. There's work to be done, with thinking, soul-searching, and prioritizing involved. Start with taking a close look at your life and the way you have being living. Many questions will come forth that you need to ask yourself and find the answers to. You must become angry committing to your fight. And you must know what you have to do. You have to unbury your clarity and your worth. Doing so will prevent you from letting yourself or anyone else treat you terribly and cheat you out of living a free and happy life.

Once you've made your decision and know your priority, then it's time to act. What will your steps be? Where will you start? Be proactive— not reactive. Do something to make a difference in your life, no matter what it takes. Risk everything to have your freedom.

Keep in mind the immigrants: Instead of being critical and uncaring toward them, we can learn from them, put our energy into understanding them, and join them. Remember Rosa Parks as well and all the others who have made sacrifices for the betterment of oppressed people. Fight for your freedom and the freedom for all. Do it for yourself, and as a result of helping yourself, you help others.

What's important in all this is to be happy with the sacrifices you will make to live your life to its fullest, so that when you die you will have no regrets for the way you have lived your life.

I've created a way to help you get started toward living a free life. This book will help you. To have and fight for your freedom in the world, you must know and understand what freedom is internally. Freedom begins with valuing yourself. To value yourself, you need to connect with yourself and know who you are. Oppressed people such as people of color and LGBTs have been targets of ridicule and hate in the world, and in turn have *internalized* those same feelings. When we internalize feelings we take on as true the beliefs others have about us, which often are negative. Internalized racism and homophobia are the chains that keep us trapped. I'm not going to go kick myself or another because somebody has kicked me; I'm going to stop and tell that person never to kick me again because I don't deserve to be kicked. This is what we need to do as a people. Kick off all the negative stuff that we carry in our souls that doesn't belong to us. Shake it off with intention, and bury it. Just imagine how things would be if we *all* did this—it would be similar to my earlier example of our soldiers boycotting being called to war. We would demonstrate by our actions that we value ourselves.

WE CAN'T BE SATISFIED

Hello world
Hello people
Hellooo!
Is anybody there?
It's time to wake up!
Your sleeping time is over.
Now, it's time to get busy.
No longer can you ignore what is happening around you.
No longer can you ignore what is happening to you.
No longer can you ignore what is happening to someone else.
No longer can you afford to turn the other cheek or look the other way.
Because this hurts everyone:
your family, your friends, the innocent child next door
and especially you.
This behavior gives one major message—
keep doing what you're doing.
Where's your pride?
Where's your fight?
Where's your allegiance?
WE CAN'T BE SATISFIED
We can't be satisfied with the way things are going.
The injustice and oppression that continue to exist.
The hate that festers and erupts into violent rages.
The bigotry—the almightiness that surrounds us all.
Who gives those people the right—the authority?
We do—the public—the quiet passive ones
—the ones who are trapped within themselves,
—the ones who are hurting on a daily basis,
—the ones who feel the injustice,
—the ones who are oppressed,
—the ones who are abused and
all the so-called allies that watch in the wings.
WE CAN'T BE SATISFIED

We're all victims.
We all are trapped.
Some literally and some as a result of fear.
Some of us hurt more than others but we're all hurting.
Some of us are aware of the hurt and some of us are in denial.
We all are short changed.
We all have to watch our backs.
We all are not at peace in our hearts and souls.
WE CAN'T BE SATISFIED
We are victims.
We are victims from the past.
We are victims of today, and tomorrow, and
we will be victims for the rest of our lives, if we don't wake up.
WE CAN'T BE SATISFIED
Some people have died fighting for our justice and our freedom.
They fought for acceptance of us.
They fought for our dignity and respect for us.
They fought for our right to have peace and happiness.
They sacrificed their personal safety
for the betterment of humankind.
They believed we have the right
to experience the American dream.
They stood up against wrong.
They stood up for us.
WE CAN'T BE SATISFIED
Don't let those deaths be forgotten.
Don't let their fight vanish from your memory.
Don't let their passion and compassion melt from your heart.
We can't forget.
There's no time.
WE CAN'T BE SATISFIED
Innocent people are being hurt everyday
while we sit passively.
Innocent people are dying
because someone didn't like something about them.
This can't go on.
This is not okay.
This is why we must act.
We must get out of our so-called comfort zones,

and take a stand.
WE CAN'T BE SATISFIED
We're in a state of urgency.
We must remember the fight.
We must open our eyes and see the light—
moving us forward out of the darkness.
Enough delay and postponing and procrastinating and
waiting for someone else to take the lead.
Each one of us must take the lead,
to continue the fight until things are right.
WE CAN'T BE SATISFIED
When will freedom reign?
When will we live as people respecting each other?
When will oppressed groups stop disrespecting
other oppressed groups?
When will we stop participating in this meaningless venture?
When will we show our worth, our value and self-respect?
When will we take back our pride, dignity?
When will we stop, and breathe and listen to our hearts,
and do what is right?
When will each and every one of us
find courage within ourselves to act?
When will we be proactive and not reactive?
When will we join together to fight for our freedom?
When will our freedom be our motivation to unite?
WE CAN'T BE SATISFIED
We must show up in droves.
Not one or two, or a hundred or a thousand.
We need everyone to do his or her part.
We must show up in numbers.
We must have all races present.
Everyone must be counted.
WE CAN'T BE SATISFIED
We have a responsibility.
We have to save lives.
First, we must take a stand.
Second, we must make a move.
Sitting back has proven time and time again,
to be harmful.

Not helpful or beneficial.
It has been a disservice.
It has beaten us down.
It has been humiliating.
WE CAN'T BE SATISFIED
WE CAN'T BE SATISFIED
WE CAN'T BE SATISFIED
As long as people are denied and demoralized
because of the color of their skin.
WE CAN'T BE SATISFIED
As long as people are rejected and dehumanized
because of their sexual orientation.
WE CAN'T BE SATISFIED
As long as people are refused
and can't afford proper medical care.
WE CAN'T BE SATISFIED
As long as people are homeless,
jobless and without food.
WE CAN'T BE SATISFIED
As long as people are not safe to walk
the streets or run in the parks.
WE CAN'T BE SATISFIED
As long as innocent children
are being abused and misused.
WE CAN'T BE SATISFIED
As long as people can't be free
to be themselves.
WE CAN'T BE SATISFIED
until each and every one of us is taking a stand
and speaking out for equal rights, and protection
for all human beings.
WE CAN'T BE SATISFIED
until all people from diverse backgrounds
are treated with respect and valued as human beings.
WE CAN'T BE SATISFIED
until we all are free from the chains that dictate our existence.

Dianna L. Grayer
June 1999

WE MUST STAND STRONG

I'm calling out to all
my sisters and brothers.
It's time that each one of us
STANDS STRONG.
We have to come out and live our lives freely.
We Must We Must

We must STAND STRONG.
We will walk with our heads up high
and our backs straight.
We will look eye to eye with those who deny us.
We Must We Must

We must STAND STRONG.
We will be truthful first to ourselves.
Accepting our gayness, and then sharing it
with our families, friends and all those we meet.
We must tell the world.
We Must We Must

We must STAND STRONG.
We will let the world know we exist.
Not just a few but many:
In all ages, all sizes, all colors, all languages and all careers.
We Must We Must

We must STAND STRONG.
We will validate ourselves each time
we tell the truth,
We will respect ourselves each time
we let someone know who we really are.
We Must We Must

We must STAND STRONG.
We will build our community
by introducing ourselves and
participating in our communities.
We will reach out and support each other.
We Must We Must

We must STAND STRONG.
We will fight back together
for our rights, for our respect, for our acceptance,
for our justice, for our equality, for our freedom.
Letting the world know we exist in proportions unfounded.
And that we're not going anywhere.
We Must We Must

We must show our faces.
We must love ourselves.
We must live healthy lives.
We must nurture our souls.
We must trust our hearts.
We must support each other.
We must encourage each other.
We must stand tall.
We must be proud.
We must live our true lives.
We must be free.

We must STAND STRONG!
We must STAND STRONG!
We Must We Must!
WE MUST STAND STRONG!

Dianna L. Grayer
9/26/00

THE HUMAN RACE

Who are we all really?
What are we all about?
Why are we here,
Living in this complex world
Where complexity reigns throughout?
Where multiculturism and differences are
degraded rather than appreciated.
Where one human insists on being superior
over another rather then equals.
Where the focus on earth is selfishness
and insensitivity, which contribute to
the destruction of the environment
rather than the preservation.
Where humans allow bigotry,
indifference and hatred to exist,
which have caused an epidemic
that's contaminating and destroying us
rather than us nurturing and embracing each other.
Where humans choose to be unhappy and miserable
in their lives instead of seeking help
to find happiness and contentment.
Where humans are angry and disillusioned—
willing to fight, but for what cause?
And for what cost?

Who knows?
No one is talking
Or is it that no one is listening?
Who holds the key to our existence?
Who holds the key to our universal existing?
Is it really survival of the fittest?
Or is it a monopoly?
Is this the way it was meant to be?

Or did we lose our course—our direction?
choosing the wrong path,
a false start indeed.
But we can get back on the starting block
With a different attitude and a different focus.
We can look into each other's souls,
connecting to our inner spirits
rather than our prejudgments.
Changing our path and making a new beginning.
One soul looking into another's soul.
One mind stimulating another's mind.
One heart touching another's heart,
Whether it be filled with happiness or sadness.
Both focused on lifting each other to the top.
To the top of the human race.
With commitment, sweat, determination,
and togetherness
We all can reach the finish line in style.

By Dianna L. Grayer
1/4/2000

DON'T TELL ME WHAT TO DO

You don't have anything better to do?
Are you using your time wisely?

Shouldn't you be home with your family loving them?
Won't you try focusing your energy on your problems, making a life for
you and your family and your relationships?
If these suggestions don't help, then find a hobby.
Do something!

Just stay out of my life.
Leave me alone.
I control my life, not you.
I'm not hurting anyone,
only loving one.
Don't tell me what to do.

Do I tell you what to do or who
you can or can't sleep with?
No I don't!
So, stay out of my life.
Stay out of my business.
Don't tell me what to do.

You can't stop me from loving myself.
No matter what you do.
I love myself!
I hope you can comprehend this,
or do you not know what this means?

Dianna L. Grayer
10/26/01

GET MAD

Listen people. We have just been insulted, degraded, invalidated, and disrespected once again by our government, which states that its stance on the "gay issue" of "Don't ask, Don't tell" will be overlooked or delayed during this time of war. LGBTs are good enough to be in the military during wartime, but before and after we're unworthy people—unable to serve our country as free, open people who deserve respect, benefits, and acknowledgment of our relationships.

Use us and then abuse us. Or abuse us and then use us. Take your choice of words. However you look at it, it is disgusting!

Supposedly our government is fighting for the freedom of the American people. This is hypocrisy and a lie! Aren't LGBTs the American people? If the government can be that uncaring and insensitive to a huge portion of its population, then who is it fighting for?

I refuse to do nothing anymore. Who do they think we are—idiots? We have to let them know we're not. We have to put an end to statements that are clearly unaccepting of LGBTs. Such declarations have to stop and not be tolerated whatsoever, because they are poison. They eat away at our core, our character. Those words are brainwashing; and when heard repeatedly, they become ingrained in a person's mind. LGBTs begin to believe they deserve what they get. When this happens to someone, the person becomes weak and defenseless, a victim. Homophobia is alive and strong, and—sad to say—internalized homophobia is just as alive and strong, sometimes even stronger.

As a Black woman I don't have the privilege of hiding. When you look at me, you see my Blackness first. People of color can't hide, even though some have tried to deny who they are and to blend into White society. But when they are discovered, it is even worse on their souls. To hate yourself and hide it, only to be discovered, is shameful: It is like hating yourself a hundred times more. Some people might see blending as survival, but I see it as the convenience of denying who you are. So stop hiding, and be true to yourself, as though it's no longer convenient. How do you feel? I hope your adrenaline is starting to kick in.

Look at what's happening in the media, in sports, show business, the music industry, corporate business, and the government.

Who are the LGBTs in the public eye?

Where is our representation?

In each of these categories, perhaps there are a few LGBTs who are out. As you think about it, you notice the lack of them. It's appalling! We have to start opening our eyes to this to see the light—no more living in the dark. It is unbelievable to think that in all the professional sports and all the different teams and all the different players, there are so few open LGBTs. How many interviews are done with a man and his partner or a woman with her partner? Now think of what the number would be if everyone who is LGBT would stand up and be counted. This also applies to the rock stars, movie stars, TV stars, government officials, doctors, lawyers, therapists, authors, CEOs, others in upper management, and all those who impact our lives. This is a reason to get angry, and I hope you're allowing yourself to do just that.

Homophobia and internalized homophobia are just that strong. They lock you out of your life. When homophobia imprisons people, the key is lost: the implication is that you don't deserve to be a member of society, and ultimately you don't deserve your freedom. The few LGBTs who are out definitely don't represent even the presumed ten percent that exists in the population. Why? Because we haven't gotten mad enough to find the key.

Even celebrities can't be free. Yes, we all need to work together to find the key that will set us free.

Heterosexuals don't have a problem getting mad and taking action. Look at how they've stopped us and what they've made us believe: that they know what's best for us, that we're not worth all the benefits they receive (marriage, domestic partner benefits), that we can't love who we want to love, that we can't be ourselves, that we shouldn't be respected, that we're nobody, and that we're undeserving of our freedom. We have to look closely, both individually and as a group, at what we have allowed to happen to us and exist around us.

Let yourself be guided by your yearning to be accepted, acknowledged, and free. Acknowledge your anger and listen to what it tells you. This is where you must start: Get stirred up and let your feelings guide you. It's time for you to trust yourself in doing the right thing to set yourself free.

We have to fight hard, working together against homophobia and internalized homophobia. The two have been hanging out too long, and it's time for the two to separate and close the door on each other. We cannot hang out with that wrong crowd. We know better, and, also, it's debilitating. We know what negativity does when you get too close to it— it brings you down, and you lose yourself. You become it. This is why we have to get mad and turn away from the negativity. We have to protect ourselves and move to the positive, and I mean *fast*.

My point is, it's time to change the status of LGBTs and others' perceptions of them in America, and hopefully the words will travel around the world.

Let's not wait to come out and celebrate only on Gay Pride Day—let's celebrate ourselves every day.

Mayor Giuliani said that, as Americans, we mustn't let the terrorists rob us of our our freedom, "Go out and live your lives as usual." A great message! And I say, Don't let homophobics rob us of our freedom. Go out and live your life freely. Embrace yourselves and be proud. We can't afford to hide any longer. Terrorists don't care. You don't know whether you're going to be here or not, so if it's your time to die, you can at least die free. Let's honor ourselves and show those who have lost everything at one point in history—Native Americans, Jews, Japanese, Latinos, Blacks and others— that their fight was not in vain. Unfortunately, these races of people continue to suffer just because of who they are. When will it stop? We need everyone to get furious enough to act. Join in the fight for your freedom, which is freedom for all. LGBTs represent all races and religions: together we can make a change. Let's at least even out the playing field.

We need more of the kind of thing that Senator Barbara Boxer did at the Bay Area Memorial the day after the WTC tragedy. What she did was positive and powerful. She was a godsend, a breath of fresh air, a drink of water when you haven't had water for days, a feeling of freedom after having been locked away for years: In front of millions, she introduced the partner of Mark Brigham (one of the many heroes and heroines who took down the hijacked plane that crashed in Pennsylvania); she acknowledged the relationship and commitment between him and Mark. And as she celebrated Mark as a hero, she validated the relationship of the two men.

I remember the moment so clearly. I didn't breathe! I was in disbelief. I couldn't believe that a gay person was being honored for serving and protecting his country. I sat still and cherished the moment. Afterward, I thought about all the other LGBTs in America who were able to witness this moment of being accepted, acknowledged, respected, and I felt true freedom. *This* is the way we should feel. We shouldn't have to feel like outcasts. We are a part of the fabric in America, members of society, human beings who want and deserve freedom. Only good can come from our being free. Acceptance will be the link that joins us all together. When we receive recognition from our government, we will be able to truly stand united in our fight for our country's freedom.

We're well into 2002, and we need to make a new commitment to ourselves and the LGBT movement. Each one of us has to get mad and join the fight. Make a vow to yourself that you will no longer block your freedom. You will no longer sit back and be abused and used by our government and others who try. Show your true self and come out, so others will know you exist and that you matter. I can see the numbers climbing. Imagine the outcome if every LGBT and every person who is oppressed would make these changes. I believe it can happen—you have to believe it, too. Remember, all we want is to be treated justly; we aren't asking for more, only for what is rightfully ours.

I can imagine how frightening it must be to contemplate coming out. But you can feel in your gut when the time is right. You owe it to yourself. All of you deserve to be acknowledged, accepted, and honored. You are a good person, and you must begin believing it now. Start talking with the one person you trust, and then move to the next and the next.

Practice telling people. Become comfortable with yourself. Start a social group with people like yourself. Ask for help and support—you can do it. You will feel better, lighter, and stronger once you set yourself free.

When you get mad, you acknowledge that something is wrong and unfair, and that you don't like it. Think about the last time you were irate. Can you remember what caused your anger? Probably something or someone offended you in some way. You didn't like what was going on. As a result of your getting mad, something happened. Perhaps your reaction motivated you to act to do something to rid yourself of your anger. This is exactly what needs to happen. Our anger moves us to act. We need to act in order to save ourselves and our lives, validate our existence, confront injustice, and experience our freedom. We have to stop turning the other cheek and act now.

If we each do our part, we will all stand free together.

May the Great Spirit guide, comfort, and protect us as we stand up for ourselves and our freedom.

GET MAD PROCESS

Use this space to get in touch with yourself and your feelings. Let yourself vent and rant and rave with your words. Don't hold back. Allow to come out whatever feelings you're harboring inside. This process allows the darkness to find the light. The light brings you clarity; that, in turn, frees your spirit.

_____

_____

_____

_____

_____

_____

_____

_____

_____

_____

_____

_____

_____

_____

_____

_____

_____

_____

_____

_____

I AM THE WIND

I am the wind that's passing you by.
I am the wind.
I am the wind that's leaving you behind.
I am the wind.

I am the wind.
I am the wind that's passing you by
Because you are afraid—afraid to be your true self.

I am the wind.
I am the wind that's passing you by
Because you have lost sight of your dreams.

I am the wind.
I am the wind that's passing you by
Because you are guided by your fears, which go nowhere.

I am the wind.
I am the wind that's passing you by
Because you have given up your life as a result of what others want,
instead of what you want.

I am the wind.
I am the wind that's passing you by
Because your voice is quiet and powerless, afraid to speak
what's real.

I am the wind.
I am the wind that's passing you by
Because you are afraid to stand up and fight for your rights, freedom,
and justice.

I am the wind.
I am the wind that's passing you by
Because you're not in touch with your thoughts, feelings, wants, and
needs, and are too afraid to admit it.

I am the wind.
I am the wind that's passing you by
Because you are trapped in a world of confusion, destruction, and
chaos and don't have the strength or courage or know
how to get out.

I am the wind.
I am the wind that's passing you by
Because you sit back passively waiting for things to happen, instead of
making things happen yourself.

I am the wind.
I am the wind that's passing you by
Because you are afraid to change—changing your negatives to
positives, and your positives to successes.

I am the wind.
I am the wind.
I am the wind that's passing you by.
Because you are afraid to change—seeing the beauty in yourself and
the beauty you will bring to the world.

I am the wind.
I am the wind that's passing you by
Because you are afraid to accept yourself, your gifts, and your
imperfections.
You are who you are.

I am the wind.
I am the wind that's passing you by
Because you are afraid to take risks and challenge yourself to say "No"
when you should, and "Yes" when you must.

I am the wind.
I am the wind that's passing you by
Because you continue to hurt yourself and others, afraid to face
your own pain and hurt.

I am the wind.
I am the wind that's passing you by
Because you are afraid to trust the process of life, to believe that you
deserve the best, the best life has to offer.

I am the wind.
I am the wind that's passing you by
Because I wasn't afraid to fail, be vulnerable, try and admit that I didn't
know all the answers.

I am the wind.
I am the wind that's passing you by.
Because I wasn't afraid to ask for help, to have my voice and stand up
for myself and what was right. I always knew
I had a purpose and worth.

I am the wind.
I am the wind that's passing you by
Because I am open, unafraid to learn, change, grow, heal, be happy,
and be loved. Because, I know I am somebody special.

I am the wind.
I am the wind that's passing you by
Because I'm not afraid to aim for the sky and to rise graciously to the
top where I will fly high high high, accomplishing all my goals and
fulfilling all my dreams.

I—am the wind.
I—am the wind.
I—am the wind—that's—passing you by.

By: Dianna L. Grayer
7/1/00

REJECTION

Rejection is not always a bad thing.
It's about you.
How you see it.
How you see yourself.
How you experience it.
How you interpret it.
And what you do with it.

A lost job.
A job you really didn't want.
The right job will come along.
A lost lover.
A lover who didn't see your beauty.
The right lover will admire you and want to be with you.
A lost friendship.
A friend who didn't value you.
The right friend will not let you down.
A lost family member.
A family member who's missing out on you.
The right family will bang down your door
because they want to see you and love you.

Rejection is not always a bad thing.
It's about you.
How you see it.
How you see yourself.
How you experience it.
How you interpret it.
And what you do with it.

Don't force things that shouldn't be.
Don't let others break you or your spirit.
Cry a little and laugh a lot.
Stay strong and you can't go wrong.
Stay focused on your course.
And you will stand with great force.

Think of balance.
If it's not, then you should stop.
Where you must be, you shall see.
Keep your head up high,
So you can fly high.

By Dianna L. Grayer
12/4/01

DISPLACED ATTENTION

First, I'm a person of color
and to you that's a disgrace.
Then I come out, letting you know I'm gay
and that's even worse.
One oppression to another.

You feel my life is an abomination.
I feel my life is wonderful.
In my reflection I see
a valued and deserving person.
Therefore, I strongly disagree with
your assessment of me and others like me.

I'm sick of you.
Get off my back.
Get off the backs of others.
Keep your negative attention to yourself.
Who are you to dictate my life and the lives of others,
on the basis that our lives don't fit into your mold?
Stop putting your doctrines on our lives.

You put so much of your energy into our lives.
So much that you're willing to sacrifice your freedom.
That same freedom you're trying to take from us.
Unlike you, my freedom is important to me.
Our freedom is important.

It appears you have some work to do.
Your attention is displaced.
You must immediately switch gears.
Fight to be free, not jailed or controlled by your fears.
Focus your energy into bettering your own life.
Not mine and others like me.

Should I remind you?
We live in the land of the free.
We live in the land of opportunity.
We can make the choice to live free.
I have. So what about you?

By Dianna L. Grayer
1/22/2000

ALL OF ME

My dreams, fantasies, wishes, aspirations,
feelings, wants, and needs
are all of me.

So, let me have them and hold them.
Don't take them away from me.
because they are me.
You take them away from me,
you take me.

I need you to let these parts of me pour like
the rain from the sky.
I need you to let these parts of me flow like
the consistent and calm of the river.
I need you to let these parts of me grow like
the freedom of the wildflowers.
I need you to let these parts of me be free like
the grace and power of a soaring eagle.

I need you to let me be me.
Encourage my self-expression.
Support my uniqueness.
Help me discover me,
all of me.

Don't block my growth and my potential to blossom
into a great me.

This will let me be happy, free, and me.
Thanks!

By Dianna L. Grayer
5/1995

HEALING YOUR EMOTIONAL WOUNDS

Healing emotional wounds is a crucial step in our movement toward freedom, both internal and external. Our emotional wounds keep us stuck and imprisoned in our chains of bondage. Internalized homophobia is the end result of other people's issues that have caused a person to not value her- or himself. Each of us must dedicate our time and energy to ourselves and commit to healing. We must spend time exploring ourselves, delving into our deepest and darkest sides. We must understand our thoughts, feelings, actions, fears, tears, and our relationship dynamics. In other words, we must understand our complete selves. This is how we set ourselves free.

We heal to regain our strength, courage, and confidence—which restores our health. Unfortunately, these important characteristics were lost somewhere on our journeys through our lives, and it's our responsibility to discover when, why, and how we lost them. This is how we will heal and regain what is rightfully ours: our ability to move freely in our lives.

Take a moment and imagine yourself feeling powerful, self-assured, and brave, ready to face anyone and any problem. Pay attention to how your body is feeling, and ask yourself, "Is this feeling worth working for?"

I hope you can begin to see and feel how your emotional wounds have blocked you from experiencing your life to its fullest. Now that you know, you can do something about it. You can make your life the way you truly want it to be. As a human being you deserve to experience all the good that life has put before you. However, this has been difficult as an LGBT in a society and country that doesn't value your existence. But things are about to change. You have been informed and enlightened. You now know that with the right information you can be different in your life. You're probably wondering, *How and where do I start?*

Well, I can understand your urgency, but to undo what time has done, takes time. There's no need to rush, because that is not how change happens.

I believe change always begins within ourselves as we understand who we are. This process takes time—so you have to be patient with yourself.

Before you start your journey to heal the emotional wounds that have prevented you from being your true self, you must receive more information about yourself. First, you must understand the process of healing: Healing doesn't happen immediately or overnight. Healing is a process no matter whether the pain or injury is emotional or physical. Remember when you cut your finger or sprained your ankle? It took time for your body to heal. Another aspect of healing is your nurturing your wound. Let's focus on your cut finger. You cleaned it and were gentle with it. You applied some medicine to promote the healing and protect it from infection. Each day you paid attention to your wound, attending to it as it healed. Just to point out, during the time you were taking care of your cut finger you were nurturing yourself. Are you imagining this?

To heal your emotional wounds the same attention is needed, but it's often a longer process depending on how deep your wound is.

You could have layers and layers of hurt and pain that have been sitting around for years because your wounds weren't taken seriously or tended to, therefore they couldn't heal.

Perhaps you didn't acknowledge your pain and avoided it altogether, so it never repaired properly. You couldn't attend to it as needed; and as a result, you lived with the pain and hurt every day of your life. You didn't value it or yourself to take the time to restore. It is said that "time heals all wounds." Does this mean that if I left my cuts, scrapes, and other injuries to fend for themselves they would have healed over time? No. Something has to happen for wounds to heal properly. Attention has to be given to the wound, or you're asking for more problems—deeper and more serious concerns. *Take a moment and think about an injury you had. Do you remember your recovery process? What did you have to do to make sure it would repair properly? Did you neglect it and it became infected? How did it finally heal?*

As for emotional wounds, I'm referring to your heart. You risk the chance of adding more layers of hurt to the already unhealed heart when you neglect your wounds. A heart that hasn't healed properly is fragile, vulnerable, and susceptible to unhealthy elements.

The wounded heart isn't protected with a strong, healthy outer layer, therefore it can't rest to gather strength and rebuild its self-confidence.

Can you remember a time when you were hurt emotionally and you felt weak and exposed and the pain stayed with you for hours, days, or even months? You just couldn't find your strength. What did you do? Did you ignore the symptoms? Then, did you notice that your situation became worse? When you're susceptible and your heart weak, other layers of hurt and pain can build on the existing wound, causing you to weaken and be sucked of your strength.

⌗❖⌗

Let's use an artichoke as a metaphor. In healing emotional wounds, the process is to pay attention and nurture each layer of hurt. Each leaf of the artichoke symbolizes a layer of pain, issues, and hurt that was ignored and left to heal on its own over time, but never did. These layers have suffocated your heart—the essence of who you are, your true self—and disturbed your mind, thus leaving your spirit abandoned. This scarred part has blocked you from fully existing, and has caused you to live in fear, settling for a life you don't want. The person you were truly meant to be has been shut down and abandoned. Your true self, your heart, has been lost in the darkness within all the layers (leaves) of pain and hurt. Your goal is to remove all the wounded layers so that you can find your heart, your true self.

Again, the process to heal each layer would be to acknowledge your wound, "*I am hurt.*" Understand it, "*Why did this happen?*" Pay attention to it by spending time and energy nurturing yourself, "*Let me sit with myself.*"

Another important step in the therapeutic process that's worth breaking down is understanding. To understand your wounds is to gain valuable information about yourself. The process of understanding is that of asking yourself probing questions to help you figure out why and how your hurt has affected your life and why you choose to ignore it. During this crucial step you get a handle on your pain and how it has controlled your life. You also learn what you need to do to prevent repeating those old behaviors that allowed the harm.

Understanding helps you prevent repeating old behaviors that allowed harm.

Although this process may sound very complex, in practice it makes sense. For example, when you get hurt, several reactions can happen: (1) you take on the pain and personalize it, meaning that you internalize the negative, critical statements from others or you misinterpret what you hear in a way that hurts yourself; (2) you become defensive and shield yourself from the healing process; or (3) you stay open, acknowledging, understanding, and working with the healing process. Most often people react one of the first two ways, which leaves them unhealed. If you didn't take the time to heal, you didn't learn the lesson you needed to learn. *Think of an experience where you didn't learn a lesson and found yourself in the same or a similar situation that caused you to experience the familiar pain from before. For example, it could be that you moved from one relationship to another relationship with the same problems, without working on the issues from the first one.*

As a result, you begin to internalize, taking the negative thoughts and feelings into yourself. These in turn work on you in ways that stop you from taking special care of yourself. *What makes a person internalize negative thoughts and feelings that were expressed by others? Why do they take them on as their own?* These questions are important to ask and answer.

When an individual internalizes unconstructive thoughts and feelings it is a reflection of that individual's low self-worth, which was low initially. Therefore, this individual didn't have a fighting chance, because her or his heart's outer layer couldn't offer protection. She or he didn't know how to reject negative thoughts and feelings from another. Let's use a house as a metaphor: The foundation of a house must be strong and solid to withstand any kind of abuse. Imagine a house with a firm foundation and a house with a weaker, unstable foundation. Which will hold up in the worst storm? Most likely the house with the stronger foundation will hold up better. Now think of a person with a strong foundation, or high self-worth/self-esteem. This person will be able to look at hurt and process it rather than internalize it as a negative reflection of himself or herself. However if a person lacks high self-worth, over years of taking on others' and his or her own negative feelings, the person's foundation becomes very weak.

I believe when an individual internalizes unconstructive thoughts and feelings it is a reflection of that individual's low self-worth, which was low initially. . . . Now think of a person with a strong foundation, or high self-worth/self-esteem. This person will be able to look at the hurt and process it rather than internalize it as a negative reflection of himself or herself.

LGBTs have experienced many years of exactly this. As a result of all the neglect, ridicule, discrimination, shame, teasing, tormenting and hate toward them, LGBTs are uncomfortable being themselves. Let's face the truth: Many LGBTs don't feel safe. Feeling insecurity at an early age obstructed the building of a solid foundation. Most children get their firm foundations from loving, nurturing, and accepting parents. Those parents mirror their children's specialness, which allows the child to grow up believing they are a worthy person. Most LGBTs didn't receive this acceptance in their families. To the contrary, many were disowned when their families found out about their sexual orientation. *Imagine a child being abandoned by her/his parent because of sexual orientation. How would this affect the child's feeling of self-worth?*

Can you relate to this? Remember your own relationship with your parents. Were they caring, encouraging and accepting of you as a child? When you came out to them? Or, would they be if you would come out to them?

Your job now is to learn to heal and replace the negative thoughts and feelings about yourself that have piled up over the years with positive thoughts and feelings. You took on pain from others and made it your problem; their words and actions were so powerful that you believed them. You blamed and hated yourself, which added more layers to your already unhealed wounds. Imagine having been molested as a child and never telling anyone. Can you imagine the self-loathing that could grow over the many years? Then, imagine that this child was LGBT and was teased, tormented, and rejected daily by family, friends, and society. This kid—now adult—already felt she or he was worthless as a result of the molestation. Imagine this child believing that being LGBT is a curse, and that the child accepts this feeling as truth about her or his worth. The process of healing takes longer in these kinds of emotionally damaging situations because of the many layers of pain, hurt, and self-loathing that have built up over the years.

Change is a part of healing, just like understanding is. First you understand, and then you move toward change. Let's assume for the moment that you were a molested child: You realize that what an adult did to you wasn't your fault, and you've learned that he or she had the problem. You understand that the molester blamed you to keep you silent and powerless. From the beginning you already were physically and mentally powerless in the situation with that adult because you were a child.

Understanding brings change.

Due to fear and the belief that's it's best to be quiet and not make waves, LGBTs are used to tolerating conditions that might not be in their best interest. This old way of avoiding calling attention to oneself has only been a detriment to LGBTs' souls. This way of thinking didn't help Blacks either—the lighter ones that is—because people can't hide the truth. You can't hide from yourself. LGBTs see that trying to hide the truth hasn't worked for them: Evil will find its prey no matter what; you just have to not want to be its prey. Change will occur in each and every one of you if you want change. Heal your scars and give the chains of bondage back to those who hate you. Your acceptance of yourself will give you strength to move forward in your life as a free person. You will suffer no longer. You will face evil head on. <u>The more of us who stand together, the stronger we will be and the better chance we will have for a victory and celebration of our freedom.</u>

Change involves hard work, but the end result is self-fulfilling and satisfying. Remember that change is slow, just like the healing process is. Think about swimming to help you understand this idea: Some people might survive after being pushed in deep, cold water, but many would drown; so people need to learn the steps of swimming and then practice them, which will help them be better swimmers.

Just like everything we do, to do better we must practice new steps we are learning. This is how we change the old to the new.

When you change, you will know you have. Many things will change about you, especially the way you think and feel about yourself and your layers of hurt. You will see yourself more positively and become more self-loving and self-accepting. Many areas of your life will be impacted— including the way you relate to family, friends, and acquaintances, and the way you see and carry yourself in your job, community, and the world. Your experience of everyday life will change. Your values, beliefs, and morals will change. The way you manage your life, bills, and health will change. Your priorities about your life will naturally be changed. The way you walk, dress, socialize, and even the way you wear your hair might change as well. This is the path of healing, a natural way of bringing you back to yourself that will manifest if you embrace the healing process. *Can you imagine yourself a transformed person? What changes would you make immediately if you had your strength and self-confidence? How would you feel?*

Your work is to know and understand why you are the way you are. How did you become the person you are? If you're angry, understand why. If you're happy, know why. If you're afraid to come out, understand why. You have the ability to connect deeply with yourself and make the necessary changes that you desire. Know that you don't have to settle for the way things now are. You have the power within to change your life. You need to heal the layers and get to the heart of the matter, and then you will change.

Once you understand why you are as you are, determine whether your reasons warrant you living the rest of your life controlled and suffocated by your layers of hurt, pain, fear, and self-hatred. If you've chosen to fight back, then it's time for you to make decisions about yourself and your life. Decisions are part of life and difficult for many. *Think about a choice you had to make and how difficult it was. Think about your decision to do your work to change your life and be your true self.*

What most people misunderstand is that when they don't actively or verbally make a decision, it does not mean they haven't made one. In actuality, they made a decision by being passive. They just didn't verbalize what they really were feeling. I want you to understand that if you make the decision to be silent or passive, giving up your opportunity to speak, *you are making a decision.* For example, when you hear a racist joke and you laugh or don't react, not saying your true feelings is a message that your audience interprets as meaning that you are okay with the racism. Your lack of action or inability to take a stand was clearly a reflection of whom you are, because this is what everyone observed. *Can you recall a situation when you allowed another to think or feel a certain way based on your silence? How did you feel knowing that you didn't speak your true feelings?*

Let's bring an example closer to issues LGBTs experience. For instance, let's say a male LGBT student was attacked at school and then a closeted LGBT teacher overheard other teachers say it was the student's fault because he deserved what he got for being LGBT. The LGBT teacher remained silent, and thus the LGBT student had no allies (straight teacher(s) or staff who would defend and support him) in the room. This is what I'm talking about. The decision was made to be silent—for whatever the reason. However, then a close-minded teacher made insensitive accusations, assuming that his or her fellow teachers were straight and all agreed, since nobody had objected. The teacher was neither challenged nor corrected nor educated, and the student had no allies and remained a victim and a target in his environment. *What if you were in this situation? What would you say or do? Would you defend the child? Would you come out? Would you educate your co-workers? Would you encourage your principal to schedule an in-service on LGBT sensitivity?*

Make a decision by verbally letting others know what you stand for. Let them know what is okay and what is not. Make decisions toward your growth and healing. Once you've made the decision to cure your emotional wounds and have committed to doing all you need to do to promote your healing, you're on your way—on your way toward accepting and honoring your true self. You will heal.

Most people are impatient and want healing to be a quick fix. Sorry, it's just the contrary. I often challenge clients to look deep in order to examine their wounds. My experience is that people don't have the patience or see the value in spending the amount of time needed to heal their injuries and themselves. Many prefer to settle and live in misery rather than face their fears, nurture themselves, and come to understand their many layers. People often don't understand that the time they would be exerting would be time they put back into themselves to better their lives.

It's amazing and mind boggling to know and think that many people consider misery their natural place in life.

Are you this type? Do you like living in misery? If yes, why and how has it benefited you? And if not, what are you actively doing to eliminate it? I so strongly believe in people and in their ability to change that it is the reason I do the work I do. If I'm unable to help someone, I don't give up with that person. I'm always open and ready to help those who want help and who are willing to trust the process of healing—no matter how long it takes. Those are the individuals who understand that they are worth their own time and energy. I let my clients know they have value and that they owe it to themselves to love and honor themselves. I let them know how important it is to learn to forgive themselves for having neglected themselves for so long. You need to learn from your past so you don't repeat it, and <u>you must do the necessary grieving that will move you on your way to a new beginning. Slow down, and let your feelings be what they are without your judging them.</u> As you do this, your feelings will flow and move through you, which will allow you to heal and open to new living. *Are you able to look at your past and point out all the times you could have done things differently? Can you cry about your losses? Are you able to forgive yourself? Can you be gentle and loving toward yourself? Are you able to say to yourself, "I'm changing my life starting right now, because I'm worthy of living a happy and free life"?* I see myself, my role, as the holder of hope. As I believe in and encourage my clients to look deep to find their answers so that they can heal, it's amazing to see them grow and change. I love to watch them feel better about who they are and how they are living life. They each begin to see themselves reflected in a different way, as a person they like and appreciate. They see their own beauty and goodness and gain an ability to move out from the darkness into the light. As they move away from misery and into a life of inner peace and happiness, they're no longer overshadowed by self-loathing and self-blaming—instead they glow with self-loving and changing. Everything about them is different, which in turn affects all areas of their lives. It's a beautiful journey to witness. *Can you imagine yourself changing your view of yourself? How would it be if you were able to feel at peace with yourself and those around you? How hard would you work for it? How proud would you feel for making the change?*

TAKING THE JOURNEY

Getting ready, preparing to take the big step.
The step that will change me and my life forever.
Consumed with fear, anticipation and moments of excitement.
Taking the journey is the commitment I have made to myself.

Taking the journey is something I must do.
First for me and only me,
but as a result of taking the journey,
my efforts and successes will touch many,
especially those close to me.

My mind races to unknown places.
My body reacts to my mind racing.
My soul responds to my mind and body's unsettling maneuvers,
letting me know that I'm on the right path, validating what I must do.
My spirit is alive, light and comforting,
also letting me know
that everything will be alright.

I must go forward with confidence.
I can't be discouraged.
I will not be derailed.
I must move myself to find my true place.
I must find out who I really am.
I want to know my true meaning and purpose.
Because the way I'm living now is not the way I want it to be.

This is why I'm taking the journey.
My journey.
My journey to the life I want and deserve.

I want to grow, change and heal.
I will sit and listen quietly to what I haven't been hearing.
I will be nurturing and loving toward myself.
I will be honest and do the right thing.
I will be healthy, taking good care of my body.
I will be accepting of new information.
I will welcome new challenges.
My heart and mind will be open.
My spirit will watch over me as
I'm taking the journey
toward a freer and happier existence.
An existence that's truly mine.

By Dianna L. Grayer
11/15/99

GOD I KNOW YOU ACCEPT ME

Oh God.
Oh God.
What am I to do?
What am I to say,
to make them know
that I'm a person
with a heart, soul, and spirit?

That I am good and wholesome.
That I am of life.
Flesh, blood, and bones.
Feelings, tears, and sorrow.
That I am who I am.
That who I am isn't wrong, grotesque or not okay.
That I'm quite the contrary.

God, I know you accept me,
Because you gave me life.
Thank you for loving me
and teaching me to open my heart
to people unlike me.

God, I hope your other children
that you gave life
those that have a problem with me
can learn your teachings as well.
Help them to open their hearts
to people unlike them.
They should see that you have,
right God?

God I know you accept me
Because you gave me life.
This is why, God,
I will continue to be me
because being myself is all I can be.
Thank you God for sharing your
strength and wisdom with me.

Dianna L. Grayer
11/12/01

SLOW DOWN

*Slow down.
Be quiet and listen to your soul.
Slow down.
Be quiet and listen to your heart.
Slow down.
Slow down.*

*We have a tendency to rush around
Staying disconnected from ourselves.
Moving to one thing and then to another.
Always trying to fill the empty space,
The empty space that's inside our hearts
and inside our souls.*

*Slow down
young girl, young boy,
young man, young woman,
slow down.*

*Be quiet and listen to your soul.
Slow down
and listen to your heart.
Slow down.*

*The answers you seek are not hard to find.
You just have to slow down
In order to see them,
to hear them.
to feel them.
And to know what to do when you find them.*

Your answers are within you.
No more filling time and space.
It's time to settle down.
It's time to run your life—not run from it.
You hold the key and
it starts with you slowing down.

Slow down
young girl, young boy,
young man, young woman,
slow down.

Be quiet and listen to your soul.
Slow down
and listen to your heart.
Slow down.

Slow down sister, brother,
mama, daddy,
slow down.

Be quiet and listen to your soul.
Slow down.
and listen to your heart.
Slow down.

Dianna L. Grayer
8/15/00

DON'T QUIT—DON'T GIVE UP

To change.
It takes time, effort, and hard work.

To grow.
It takes time, attention, and enduring discomfort.

To remodel a house.
It takes time, consistency, and hard work.

To keep the landscape groomed.
It takes time, commitment, and energy.

To be a parent.
It takes time, patience, and caring.

To have a career.
It takes time, dedication, and determination.

To have a social life.
It takes time, effort, and energy.

To undo negative messages and faulty beliefs.
It takes time, willingness, and understanding.

To heal childhood pain.
It takes time, patience, caring, and commitment.

No matter what I do,
*It's in **my power** to make it happen.*
This is my life and my life is important.
I must make a commitment because I want to see it through, and I
know it will take time, patience, attention, caring, willingness, effort,
energy, hard work, enduring discomfort, consistency, dedication,
understanding, and determination.
        So,
            DON'T
                QUIT—
                    DON'T
                        GIVE
                            UP.

SOUL-SEARCHING

Soul-searching is exactly what it says, searching your soul. It's time! I believe people in general don't take time out of their day-to-day lives to be quiet and listen to their souls. Their lives are *just too busy*. This is what I hear so often from people. Your most important investment is *you* and most people don't understand this concept. It means you should never be too busy for yourself—you come first. Ultimately, all we have is ourselves. When you don't take the time to connect with yourself, destructive things start to happen. *Think about your life. What happens when you're overloaded, overwhelmed, or too busy—when you feel there's not enough time in your day?* As I write this I feel the stress and the heaviness weighing me down. I feel uncentered and my body aches. If I remain in that place, I get sick; I become more accident prone, more easily irritated, and I say things I don't mean. I turn short tempered and become forgetful and preoccupied. I am unable to concentrate or listen. And the list goes on. Are you feeling me? Yourself?

There comes a time when a person has to claim herself or himself as a priority: This means doing what is in his or her own best interest. By "investing in yourself" I mean spending quality time with yourself. And I'm not talking about watching TV alone!—I'm talking about checking in with yourself.

Soul-searching involves looking deep into yourself and your life. It's a self-exploration process. Take the time to look inside yourself and see what work needs to be done so you can live freely. This is your opportunity to focus on the problems that you have overlooked or ignored. It's the time to ask yourself the big questions: Many avoid these questions at all costs because they make you truly look at yourself and how you are living your life. These questions stir up feelings that have been neglected and suffocated. Many people feel powerless when it comes to their feelings, so they turn away from them. But I want you to know you're *not* powerless. Unfortunately, many people would rather self-medicate than confront their feelings. By *self-medicate* I mean numbing the pain with drugs and alcohol. Some other ways to avoid oneself are preoccupation with sex, spending money, TV, video games, Internet, and overworking. Take a moment now and think about what **you** do when you don't want to deal with conflicts, hurt, or disappointment. *Does what you do ever get rid of the problem? How do you feel afterward?*

Soul-searching will launch you on your journey to change your life. Your taking time to stop, look, listen, and learn says a lot about you and your commitment to yourself. For LGBTs to gain the respect and acceptance we deserve, we all must do our part. Your part is to get to know yourself. When each one of us has learned to accept, love, honor, and respect ourselves as LGBTs, then it will be much easier for society and our government to accept us. It begins with us. Change happens when people make it happen. *Remember when you were a kid and were harassed by a bully? What worked? Did you run? Or were you finding a way to stand up to the bully? Perhaps you asked for help. Something had to happen for the bully to stop—you took some kind of action.* This is how it is today. We have to take action. When we begin to put time and energy into healing ourselves, the outcome will be significant. We will be stronger, more self-assured, and will feel more worthy. We will be grounded individuals ready and able to fight for our rights. Each person will be better equipped to face the bullies, all those people who threaten your sense of worthiness and freedom.

So, in short, you have to see what's broken in order to know what to fix. What you put into yourself is what you will get out. Don't let your denial stop you any longer. (*Denial* is when you think everything is fine when we all know something is most definitely wrong.) Sometimes a person's denial is so strong that he or she is convinced that everything is okay. In some extreme cases of denial, a person hears they have a month to live and they think it's a lie. Or a person is almost a skeleton due to lack of healthy eating, but they say they're fine and eating well. Or they say they're happy when everything in their life is crumbling around them. Or they claim their relationship is perfect, but because the bruises show it's apparent they are in an abusive relationship. Don't let your denial prevent you from seeing the truth. Spend the time to find out what is really important to you. Enough already, it's time to come home to what matters—you!

If you're not in denial, then it must be fear that is stopping you. Fear manifests in many ways. I once heard a teacher say that she didn't want to come out of the closet at her school because she didn't want her co-workers to see her as a "gay teacher," and she was afraid they wouldn't take her seriously purely as a teacher. This teacher's assumption was that if she were assumed to be straight, she would be respected more. Hello! Wake up. This is internalized homophobia, to think that you are not deserving of respect. So again, we have to change our thinking and recognize that we deserve to be a free people. This lesbian teacher is a teacher just as are her fellow straight teachers: They are all teachers, and one is no better than the other. To think otherwise comes from fear, fear of being our true selves. And this is why it's important to soul-search: You will be able to know when you're rationalizing and when you're honest. You will know what changes need to take place in you so you can build your self-confidence and self-esteem and become true to yourself. Both you and this teacher can be real.

It's important to learn why you allow your fear to suffocate you and block you from fighting for your life. As you can see with the example about the teacher, the mind is a powerful tool. It is so powerful that it can make a person convince her- or himself of something that's not true.

Your fears keep company with one another, which keeps you stuck in your trepidations—such as the terror of being assaulted, harassed, demoted, losing your job, or being ostracized or rejected by a family member and/or a friend. Believing your worries, you build up your self-doubts.

The truth that you must face and come to terms with is,
Fear Is a Frame of Mind and You Must Overcome Yours.

Once you learn to love and accept the person you are, you will be better able to deal with your fears, and eventually they will disappear. If you lose your job, you will be confident to find another that will be better suited for you. If you lose a friend or family member, you will be able to find friends and family who will love you regardless of your sexual orientation.

Most of the time people who are confident and strong are less likely to be made targets. Therefore, don't let your fears prevent you from living your life to its fullest.

I encourage you to spend more time soul-searching—which means listening to and understanding yourself and what your existence is about. Remember, you're investing in yourself; you will benefit from your time and effort. It doesn't require a lot: Beginning with only fifteen minutes a day would be effective; however, an hour or more would be better. With that hour you can save yourself and begin to heal your soul. And you've already read about how important the healing process is.

❖ℋ❖*COOBODAY*❖ℋ❖
(Grant strength, courage, and guidance)

Oh God, my rock and my redeemer,
Give me strength and courage.
Let me feel love in my heart.
Secure inner peace in my soul.

Straighten my back and
have it be flexible and strong.
Lift my shoulders
and have them be broad and wide.
Heal my heart and
have it beat with openness and purpose.
Sharpen my eyes and
have me see clearly and far.
Brace my legs and
have them carry me the distance.

Ground my feet and
have them move gracefully and free.
Focus my mind and
have it be smart and wise.
Secure my arms and hands and
have them be my support and balance.
Join my mind, body, and soul and
have them be unified and whole.

Let me feel you with me.
Let me feel your presence.
Let me feel your touch.
With your help and my efforts and dedication
toward my healing and change, I will be successful.
Thank you, God, my rock and my redeemer,
for your spirit and your blessings.

COOBODAY

Dianna L. Grayer, 1996

Getting started on your journey inside yourself. Find a private, quiet place to be with yourself. Make this place your personal healing area. You might want to create an altar and fill the area with belongings that are special and important to you—for example, rocks, driftwood, power animals, angel cards, religious symbols, photos, baby pictures. Candles, sage for smudging to cleanse the area, incense, and soft instrumental music create a healing atmosphere as well. Have a journal, pencil, pen, and colored pencils available for you to use to write and draw about thoughts and feelings that are generated during your time alone.

After setting up your area, lie or sit comfortably. (I always lie on my bed or create an area on the floor with a blanket.) Begin by clearing your head—removing all your thoughts. Focus your attention on yourself. Breathe deeply, inhaling through your nose and into your stomach and then exhaling through your mouth. The deep breathing will help you relax. (You can put one hand on your stomach and another on your chest. Your chest stays steady while your breath goes deep into your belly.) Pay attention to your breathing, noticing the rise and fall of your stomach. This will help you clear your mind by focusing your awareness on your breathing. As you continue your breathing, send each in-breath into another part of your body. As you do this, notice each area of your body including your face, neck, chest, stomach, knees, legs, and feet. Give attention to your entire body, and spend more time in any painful or tight areas. Don't rush this process. Spend several seconds in each area. *As you travel through your body, what do you notice and feel? In some places do you feel sadness or the need to cry? How is it to be with yourself this way?*

Once you're relaxed, begin to think about your life and how you are living. Ask yourself some questions that help you move deep inside: *What has been heavy on my mind and heart? Am I happy? What do I want? What are my needs, and are they being met? What am I afraid of? Why is it hard for me to take care of myself?* After you've asked the questions and they have rested in you for a while, get your journal and write and draw what you feel and see within. No pressure. Don't try to correct your words or worry about spelling or grammar. Your job is to write and let yourself be free. Don't hold back. Let whatever is in you out. Set it—and yourself—free.

This time you are spending in connecting with yourself is so valuable. After a short while, you will see and feel the difference. Just remember to be patient with yourself. This is your time to nurture your soul. Don't be talked out of your time with yourself. Don't sacrifice your*self* for others or for things. In this way you begin to honor, love, value, and accept yourself.

)(❖)(

Below are more questions to help you think about yourself and your life. This process will allow you to continue learning, healing, and changing. Each day, sit in the quiet space you created for your healing, and write. Please don't try to answer all these questions in one sitting. Healing is a slow process, so you need time in-between sessions to let your new discoveries settle within your mind, heart, body, and soul. Take only a few questions per day to write and explore. You most likely will need more space to write in than the lines that follow, so continue in your private journal.

It's important for you to know yourself.
You are worthy of your time.

As you work through the questions that follow, jot down your own questions that emerge. They will become useful tools for your self-exploration as you become accustomed to searching within. They will assist you in removing the layers that block you from living free.

What feelings are with me most of the time?_____

_____

_____

_____

_____

_____

What do I often think about?_____

_____

_____

_____

_____

If I were to focus my attention on my heart, what would it say?_____

_____

_____

_____

_____

_____

_____

_____

_____

_____

What makes me mad? Share a time when I became very angry._____

_____

_____

_____

_____

_____

_____

_____

_____

What makes me happy? Share a situation when I was extremely joyful._____

_____

_____

_____

_____

_____

What makes me sad? Share a situation when I was extremely heavy-hearted._____

_____

_____

_____

_____

_____

_____

What do I often complain about?_____

_____

_____

_____

_____

_____

_____

_____

What motivates me? What do I like to do that brings me joy and satisfaction?_____

_____

_____

_____

_____

_____

What do I dislike about my life?_____

_____

_____

_____

_____

_____

_____

_____

_____

_____

What do I like about my life?_____

_____

_____

_____

_____

_____

_____

_____

What is my purpose and my meaning?_____

_____

_____

_____

_____

_____

_____

_____

How would I describe myself?_____

_____

_____

_____

_____

_____

_____

_____

_____

How would someone else describe me?_____

_____

_____

_____

_____

_____

_____

_____

Am I kind and gentle toward myself? Explain._____

_____

_____

_____

_____

_____

_____

Do I take care of myself emotionally, physically, and mentally? Explain.

_____

_____

_____

_____

_____

_____

_____

Do I sacrifice myself for others? Explain and describe one example.

_____

_____

_____

_____

_____

_____

_____

What do I do when I can't cope with my life? Does it help me? Describe a time when I just couldn't handle life._____

_____

_____

_____

_____

_____

_____

Do I take responsibility for my actions, or do I blame others? Explain._____

_____

_____

_____

_____

_____

_____

_____

Do I respect myself and take myself seriously?_____

_____

_____

_____

_____

_____

_____

Do I have supportive people in my life? Tell about three people I can count on._____

_____

_____

_____

_____

_____

_____

_____

What changes do I want to make in myself? _____

_____

_____

_____

_____

_____

_____

_____

_____

What changes do I want to make in the way I live my life?_____

_____

_____

_____

_____

_____

_____

_____

_____

Do I give up quickly on myself and on things I want, or do I fight for what's important to me? Explain._____

_____

_____

_____

_____

_____

How has my childhood influenced who I am today?_____

_____

_____

_____

_____

_____

_____

_____

_____

_____

How would I describe my life?_____

_____

_____

_____

_____

_____

_____

_____

_____

Who is controlling my life—me? My parents? My partner? My fears?
Someone or something else?_____

_____

_____

_____

_____

Who is that one person I would like to tell my honest feelings to if only I weren't fearful? What would I say and why?_____

_____

_____

_____

_____

_____

_____

_____

Am I open or not about my sexual orientation? Explain why. _____

_____

_____

_____

_____

_____

_____

_____

Have I, or has someone close to me, been treated wrongly because of being LGBT? Describe an incident._____

_____

_____

_____

_____

_____

_____

_____

How do I feel knowing that I am hated by so many people and am not accepted?_____

_____

_____

_____

_____

_____

_____

_____

_____

How do I feel about the unfairness and injustices LGBTs face every day? Explain._____

_____

_____

_____

_____

_____

_____

How badly do I want to live freely in myself and in America? Explain.____

_____

_____

_____

_____

Do I feel worthy of my freedom? Explain._____

_____

_____

_____

_____

_____

_____

_____

How would I feel if LGBTs were accepted members of society? Explain.

_____

_____

_____

_____

_____

_____

_____

How would the world be without people who hate? _____

_____

_____

_____

_____

_____

_____

_____

_____

Do I hate or dislike others (races, religions, cultures, lifestyles)? How do I feel about diversity? Explain. _____

_____

_____

_____

_____

_____

_____

Do I think the process of soul-searching was beneficial for me and would be for others? Explain._____

_____

_____

_____

_____

_____

_____

_____

What will I do with my newfound knowledge?_____

_____

_____

_____

_____

_____

_____

_____

Do I feel my time was well spent?_____

_____

_____

_____

_____

_____

_____

_____

_____

_____

Do I feel I want to be different in my life as a result of understanding myself better? If no, explain. If yes, what am I planning to do differently?

_____

_____

_____

_____

_____

_____

_____

_____

_____

_____

_____

_____

_____

_____

Other Questions to Explore

As you have learned, there are many more questions to be answered. Take the time to answer all your questions. Get them out of your mind and body and out in the open for clarity. Write, learn, and understand. This time you spend with yourself is valuable.

Applaud yourself for making the commitment to look into your heart and soul, because you shall reap the benefits.

_____

_____

_____

_____

_____

_____

_____

_____

_____

_____

_____

_____

_____

_____

_____

_____

As a matter of fact, you already have begun looking into your heart and soul. And you are better acquainted with yourself as a result.

It's like prevention work. You've saved yourself a lot of unnecessary pain just by learning about who you are. From this point on, you are a different person—more in tune with your needs and desires—which will move you on the right path for achieving the life you want. Denial and fear now are merely words with little or no charge. You are clearer about yourself and what you stand for. Your path has been made apparent, and you no longer are being directed by others.

Now you are the director of your life.

Your new leadership will guide you forward

in your renewed, open, and free life.

I WILL NOT STOP MY LIFE

My pain and hurt from my past
Doesn't make up who I am.
I will not stop my life
because of sorrow and anger.

Don't sit back and do nothing.
Fight back for your life.
Opportunities awake you.
You just have to believe.

If you're content on being a follower
until you're ready to become a leader,
then follow the positives
Eliminating all, I mean all, the negatives.

I have to move my life
being all I can be.
I am worth it—You are worth it.
I am somebody and
you are somebody too.

Cry, get it out.
Make your comeback.
Take back your life.
Become the leader that you are.
Live your life to its fullest.

Dianna L. Grayer
2/15/2000

REMOVING THE CHAINS
OF BONDAGE

I've shared much about the healing process and what you need to do to change your life—but I haven't given you many tools to help you on your journey. You have been patient, which is a good sign of your development. The process was difficult, and you stayed with it. Hooray to you. Now, you're about to put into practice tools that will change your life forever. These tools will help you become the person you desire to be.

In removing your chains of bondage, you will make a big statement to yourself and others and you will communicate a stronger, more confident, and wiser person. You have learned to be kind and nurturing toward yourself as you confront your life; now it is time to also learn to protect your healing from those who are not supportive.

Don't let others take you away from what's important—you.

If you learn and use each of the following tools in your life, both you and how you live your life will change. As with anything, it's up to you what you do with this information. If your goal is to transform, then you will do what you need to do in your day-to-day living to encourage positive change. Your dedication and commitment will be evident as you move toward your deserved freedom. You can exclaim to the world, "I'm on my way! No more chains! No more bondage! No more fear! No more neglecting myself! Free at last, free at last!"

Exercise Positive Self-Talk. This is a style of talking to yourself with a voice that comes from within you and is loving, gentle, and nurturing. This voice is your best friend. It believes in you, and it forgives you when you make mistakes. This voice always encourages. Whenever you're in doubt, fall back on your positive self-talk—it really works. Your goal is to replace all your negative thoughts, feelings, and judgments with positive ones. This is the way to develop your self-esteem and self-worth. Tell yourself positive messages every day using "I" statements. Using "I" statements will bring the messages home because you will own what you say. For example, for starters, try saying, "I'm a good person and deserve to be happy and free."

Whenever you catch yourself being judgmental or negative toward yourself, immediately reword your thoughts into a positive statement, and say it three times out loud. People sometimes think that their inner critic, the voice that "beats them up" is the more truthful voice. Not so! Our thoughts and feelings are extremely intertwined, and it's the nature of our inner critic to feed us misinformation that hurts us. These are old scripts that keep us off course. If you think your positive thoughts are less true than your self-hurtful thoughts, remember that in each moment your feelings are influenced by your thoughts, and you do have the choice to enjoy your life and treat yourself with kindness. At first, you might feel odd thinking of yourself positively; but in time, you will become comfortable with the new you. So say goodbye to the critic.

Change Your Language. People often don't recognize how their language affects their lives. I know it does. I'm referring to two kinds of language: one is derogatory language (belittling and insulting), and the other is heterosexism. Words hurt. As a foster parent, I prohibit my foster children from saying words like "stupid" or "dummy"; and they are forbidden from using vulgar language, especially "faggot" or "nigger" and other insensitive names. Clean up your mouth. Be aware of what you say about yourself and others. You don't have to be cruel to get your point across. Derogatory and vulgar words keep negativity trapped inside your heart and soul.

Know what it means to be heterosexist: *Do you assume that everyone is straight? Have you asked a female teenager whether she has a boyfriend, or a male teenager whether he has a girlfriend?* Pay attention to your assumptions. At a party we went to, a lesbian asked our foster daughter whether she had a boyfriend. This made our daughter very uncomfortable: The dating pressure was one aspect, but what if she were lesbian? Don't assume. We should know better and remove our tunnel thinking.

I play basketball, and every time I hear another woman say, "man to man" when it's so easy to say, "player to player," I feel as though someone is driving a stake through me. All the *man*-ending words need to be replaced with words to represent both sexes: mail carrier, police officer, firefighter, two-person raft, and the like. Support women—we do exist. Who created our language anyway? If even we LGBTs aren't willing to make some conscious changes, how can we expect straight America to change its consciousness to ever have our rightful place in society?

Discover Your Self-Esteem and Self-Worth. Self-esteem is your foundation. It carries you through life. "Self-esteem is the ability to value one's self and to treat oneself with dignity, love and reality," as said by psychotherapist-author Virginia Satir (*The New Peoplemaking*, 2d ed. [Mountain View, Calif.: Science and Behavior Books, 1988], 22). Building your self-esteem is your immediate goal. You begin as you stop hating and blaming yourself. You have the power within to change your beliefs about yourself and love yourself.

When you matter to yourself, you will show yourself positively to the world. Regarding yourself as worthy will move you positively in your life.

By focusing your attention on yourself, you will be taking care of yourself—which will naturally heal you and build your character. Positive self-talk changes the way you see yourself and encourages your self-love and sense of self-worth—these are your new priorities. In turn, increased self-appreciation will protect you from wrongdoing, because when you love yourself you will not do things to harm yourself nor will you let others harm you. The negative energy you once carried will no longer be attracted your way. Self-love guides you on your journey through life with strength and confidence.

Connect With Your Inner Child. Tuning in to your inner child is key to your existence. I use the *inner child* as a metaphor. It is a concept that helps people do the reparenting work necessary to claim their lives.

Embracing a relationship with your inner child is so important. Many people initially have a difficult time understanding the inner child metaphor and process. However once they begin delving in to doing the work with their own inner child, they quickly understand the value of the process, which is about looking back at your childhood and examining how you were treated, how you felt from that treatment, and who you became in response to it. Childhood is the time when people first encountered heartbreak as a result of some kind of pain: whether emotional, physical, sexual, and/or verbal. And they may well have experienced neglect, rejection, abandonment, and/or loss. These early experiences cause people to react in ways that are unhealthy because they felt unloved and damaged, rather than special and valued. As a result, their lives took a turn on a path away from their truest course.

Connecting with your inner child is about healing the pain you suffered as a child so that as an adult you can move freely on your rightful path. This healing process is one of reparenting. You give to the "child within you" the attention and nurturance she or he needed but did not receive. You comfort and nurse the child to becoming strong, healthy, and confident, able to live her or his life to its potential. By being encouraging, positive, accepting, and loving to your inner child, you create the safe space in which the necessary grieving can take place for you to heal.

You begin to honor that little child you once were, and you give all the love and attention he or she missed as a child. As a result, the child feels safe—and you feel committed to keeping it this way. You begin to feel a shift in yourself that feels good and enables you to live the rest of your life in honor of and respect for that child. Holding that child in the highest esteem, always, you then live your life for her or him. This child wants to be free to live—no longer wants to be punished or hurt—that was the life of the past.

Get an 8" x 10" photo of yourself and spend time becoming acquainted with your inner child; reassure him or her that you will take good care of the child beginning today. Connecting with your inner child definitely will raise your self-esteem and self-worth. Love and cherish her or him, and reap the benefits. Get ready to soar high! high! high!

My inner child is with me, always. All that I do is in honor of her. She is loved and celebrated every day. I don't do anything that would hurt or jeopardize her integrity and self-respect. I love her so much, and we both feel great!

Practice Self-Awareness. It's important that you become more alert to yourself. You must begin to notice everything about yourself, including how you think and feel about yourself and others. *How do you feel about being alone? How do you feel when you're with each person you spend time with? How do you feel afterwards from having been with that person?* Always notice how you respond to different situations. Notice when you speak out and when you don't. Notice when you are happy, angry, or disappointed. Pay attention to what you eat and drink, and how much or how little you consume. Notice how you carry yourself and how you function in your life. Parts of who you are need to be changed. First you must be aware of what is not working; then you can work toward changing those aspects of yourself and your life. The only way you will know is by your vigilance. The more self-aware you become, the more connected you will be to yourself.

Be Selfish. Many people who are dealing with emotional hardship and have been victims sacrifice their own needs for the sake of others. No more. You can't sacrifice yourself for someone else's feelings. You give and give and yet receive disrespect again and again. This only causes you to hurt, become angry at, and devalue yourself. The cycle of self-destruction continues. It doesn't work anymore—and it never really did. Every time you have put others before yourself and ahead of your own feelings, you only caused yourself more upset and pain. Now is the time for you to let others know that you—just like they—are worthy and have wants and needs, likes and dislikes, too. Share your opinions and your points of view; this shows that you like yourself, and liking yourself is very positive.

People who are used to putting others before themselves often feel that they are deserting others when they begin to concern themselves with their own well-being. On the contrary: People who care about themselves and treat others with similar respect (remember the good old golden rule?) serve as inspirations and models for those whose lives they touch. They are the people we feel so good around because they are whole and healthy. They are the ones who have some reserve energy and compassion to give us because they've nourished their own spirits.

Be Honest. Be candid with yourself and others. It's so important for you to learn to be forthright, but it will take a lot of practice. So many people are unable to say what they feel or what they want and need. Beginning to trust yourself will help you be honest. It's time for you to face yourself and your truths. When you find yourself struggling internally, stop and pay attention. Listen to what you are feeling and say it out loud. Practice this every day and every time you get the weird feeling you get in your gut when you aren't being truthful. Let people see and hear you. Tell them who you are and show them how proud you are to be yourself. Being direct is freeing. Through honesty you will grow and be secure with your life.

Heal Your Pain. A whole chapter was dedicated to the healing process because it is a crucial part of the movement toward your freedom. You have to look deep within and remove the layers that have kept you afraid and restrained in your movement in life. When you confront your pain and fears, you become unstoppable—there's nothing holding you down or back. You're free to move and go about your life on the path you choose for yourself, not the path others have chosen for you. You become the leader, not the follower, of your pain. If your pain is so deep that you can't set yourself free on your own, seek professional help. There is nothing to be ashamed of in seeking help; you deserve good support and guidance. Don't let yourself or anyone stop you from living the life you deserve.

Face Your Fears. Fears you hold keep you stuck, chained, and bound in limbo, and they prevent you from following your dreams. Facing your fears is a process—it doesn't happen overnight. Now is the time to begin confronting your fears so they will no longer take you down a path that's not yours. Your fears have blurred your vision and have stopped you from reaching out into your future. When you discover your worth, it will give you the strength and confidence to fight for what you deserve in your life.

Confronting others is one fear that's frightening for most. Yet, confrontations don't have to be a scary thing: The truth is the truth. Tell people what you feel. Say whatever you need to say for the situation to be better so that you can move forward. For example, "I don't like it when you poke fun of me. And I don't want you to do that anymore."As you face your fears, you restore your personal power by respecting yourself and what's important to you. Make a list of all your fears, and overcome each and every one of them. Make a step-by-step plan describing exactly what you will be doing to overcome your fears. (See "Challenge" on page 97 in this book.) Be kind and patient with yourself on every attempt. You will be amazed watching your own change and growth—you will feel good inside and so much better able to enjoy your life.

Eliminate the Negatives. Your goal is to eliminate all the negatives in your life, which includes negative people as well. You have no room in your life for them. It's time to do some spring-cleaning. You need to get rid of all the stuff in your life that is not benefiting you. If you're drinking too much alcohol, it's time to stop. If you're doing drugs, it's time to stop. If you're overeating or undereating, it's time to eat healthier. If you're not exercising, then it's time to start. No more of your time will be wasted on negativity. Clean up your language and all your negative thoughts and feelings about yourself and others, too. Replace your negative attitudes with positive energy. Rid yourself of self-doubt and fears. Rid yourself of anger.

Getting rid of your anger is different than getting mad. Getting mad is about taking action and gaining control of your human right—your freedom. Getting rid of your anger is a process toward eliminating the negative aura you carry within yourself. So many people carry anger with them—both internally (through self-hurting behaviors and/or self-hatred) and externally (through abusing people, animals, and things). Far too much anger, violence, and emotional abuse is going on in the world, and LGBT families and relationships account for part of it, especially when it comes to anger toward self. Anger keeps a person stuck, unable to live freely and peacefully.

When you understand the root of your anger, learn anger management skills and keep a feeling journal for support, you can begin to work on healing that part of your life. For example, internalized homophobia causes people to carry anger toward themselves or toward others. The experiences of having been abused as a child or neglected or abandoned or rejected or criticized all cause a person to be angry. Once you do the personal work to understand the root of your anger, new opportunities will open up for you: One change will be that you will learn to communicate more honestly and openly about yourself and your feelings. This way *you* will be the driving force in your life, instead of your anger driving you.

All of the negative influences you carry around prevent you from living a peaceful, healthy, happy, and free life. They blur your vision and numb your existence, which prevents you from living your life to its fullest. Eliminating your negatives will also change you into a much happier and freer person. Your heaviness will melt away and will be replaced by a gentle and special spirit. Let your true spirit surface.

Develop Positive Support Systems. Many LGBTs have been disowned or shamed by their immediate family; thus, the family they were born into caused them the greatest pain. A time comes when, painful as it is to think of doing so, you must let go of something that is out of your control. You can't control what others do, but you can control what you do. On your journey to loving and respecting yourself, eliminate all the people in your life who are unsupportive and critical of you for whatever reason.

Rejection is not always a bad thing: Why would we want people in our lives who don't want us? We want people in our lives who do want us.

And as you want more, you will get more—you will find you demand more for yourself because you recognize that you deserve it. It is time to say good-bye to those who refuse to see you as you are. You must let them know that you merit being supported, loved, and respected; and if they can't treat you with that regard, then you must find those who will. Remove your chains and liberate yourself. You can create your own family. Surround yourself with positive and accepting people, and stay away from people who don't validate you. You are valuable and worthy and it's time you start believing it and showing that to others. You can do it!

Enjoy Spirituality. If you lack spirituality, then find it. Spirituality is different for each individual: Some have a religious faith; some find holiness in nature; others hold a belief and attitude about how they conduct themselves in their lives; and yet others find guidance through their inner child. I experience spirituality in my connection to something greater than myself, God, and also in my connection to my inner child, a connection that is powerful and strong. I am who I am because of her and also through the support, guidance, and love of God, who I refer to as the Great Spirit. I experience a goodness in myself, a grounding in myself, a feeling of wholeness.

Spirituality is about goodness—it really isn't about anything negative. Following spirituality, you always move toward what is positive and good. It's a feeling of freedom. Pray or ask for guidance, and be vigilant so you can receive it. Pay attention to what makes you feel good and complete inside your heart and soul.

When you have made the connection to your spirituality, you will know it because you will feel different than before about yourself, other people, and the world at large. You will find that you stop running and stop being afraid. Instead, you will relax and participate more fully in your life. You reap these benefits when you put time and energy into healing yourself. You need to be quiet and listen, and the answers will surface. Then you will know. So slow down and become acquainted with yourself and your spirituality. **Find your wholeness—you shall find peace.**

Follow Your Dreams. All the soul-searching and connecting with yourself that you will do will cause you to see your life differently—as though a blindfold were removed from your vision. The world will suddenly become available to you as the weight you've carried around lightens. Now the effort to reach your dreams doesn't feel so enormous. If you want to do something, do it anyway. Live each day tuned in to your spirit, and follow it—it will take you where you really want to go. Don't waste any more time procrastinating or being afraid. Don't let others' negativity or disbelief prevent you from doing what you want.

If you believe you can, you will.

You can do it! Ask for help and guidance, and you shall get all you ask for. You merely have to have faith and believe in yourself and your dreams. Go get 'em!

Find Your Happiness—Each of the following will lead you to happiness: ❖ Accept, love and honor yourself. ❖ Take care of your needs. ❖ Respect yourself, others and the earth. ❖ Be honest in all areas of your life. ❖ Show your true self, and tell people your feelings. ❖ Be kind and nurturing toward yourself and others. ❖ Eliminate all the negatives in your life. ❖ Change your language. ❖ Trust yourself, and follow your dreams. ❖ Find your inner peace. ❖ Develop a positive support system. ❖ Take risks and challenge yourself. ❖ Stand up and demand your freedom. Doing all this will make you and your life a priority—you will be very happy.

More Tools To Help. The following are only a few of the additional things you can do to help yourself on your journey to a happy, free existence: ❖ Use **Journaling** to tap into your day-to-day feelings and thoughts. Move that stored stuff out of your system, and bring it to the light. ❖ Lighting **candles and incense** can enhance the pleasant, relaxing atmosphere while you write in your journal. Candlelight and incense can be calming and helpful when you do creative healing work such as drawing, other art activities, and poetry. Often images surface when people write, and they want to draw them—and poems often come to people naturally, and they want to capture them. (The first book I wrote, *Journaling: Getting to Know Yourself,* can be instrumental in helping you move deeper inside yourself..) ❖   Listening to **music** is wonderful. You may have some music that takes you deep inside yourself. If so, listen to it while you spend time alone with yourself. New Age genre works wonderfully, especially Native American flute. Most of the music used by massage therapists will work. Play music, and let it take you on a journey inside yourself. ❖   Having **hobbies or interests** is important. Get involved in something that you like and that brings you joy. ❖ **Laughing** is healing. Always find time to laugh. You've got to have a sense of humor to survive. Relax! Have Fun! ❖ Going on **nature walks** is very relaxing and healing. Explore some nature trails, and admire the beautiful land that surrounds you. I find the **beach** a place where I can set myself free. When I'm at the ocean, my heart and mind are open to receiving new knowledge. Schedule time in your week to be in nature so that you can relax and free yourself. It's a good time and place to practice breathing deeply, too. Doing so will help you receive new insights. Sit and think about your life: *Where are you and where are you going?* ❖ Cultivating the **practice of sharing your feelings** is an important skill to learn. Share your feelings whenever you can: Find a person with whom you feel comfortable. Choose someone who is willing to help you feel more comfortable expressing your feelings. Tell this person exactly what you need them to do. You might want to use a tape recorder or video camera to give you another level of feedback. A mirror, too, can be helpful, because you can learn about yourself by seeing yourself as you share. Always use **"I" statements** when you share, "I feel. . ." Talking this way will help you own your feelings. The more comfortable you are with yourself, the more comfortable you will be when you're sharing your feelings with others. Think of the times you wished you could have shared your true feelings. Let this motivate you. ❖ Using a little portable **tape recorder** as you walk in nature, or are out on a drive, can be a helpful tool for clarifying and brainstorming feelings and thoughts, and you can even send the tape to someone you want to share your feelings with. Let yourself talk uncensored! You can even create a typed letter of your recorded words and send it as a letter if you so choose. ❖ Find **professional help** if you need or want it. If your life seems out of reach, seeking help from a professional therapist can help you get your life back on track.

You deserve to feel good. Think of using these tools as investing in yourself. That's what this whole book is about. Think of your needs, and take care of yourself.

LOOK AT ME

Take a good long look at me.
Really look at me.
I am beautiful.
Take a good long look at me.

I am happy to be who I am.
I love my skin color.
I am content with my type of hair.
I choose to love who I want.
I love my body and
all the feelings it brings me.
Even the pain allows me to grow.
I have a heart of gold.

I am proud and know
that I am special.
I'm strong and independent.
Capable of learning and becoming greatness.
I trust myself, my thoughts and feelings.
Because at the end of any situation.
There is only me.
I have to be good to myself.
I have to respect myself.
I have to take care of me.

I don't have a problem with myself.
I don't have a problem with who I am.
I don't have a problem with how I look.
Because I love me and accept all of me.
I am okay.
Really, I am more than just okay.
Take a good long look and you shall see.

Take a good long look at me.
Really look at me.
I am beautiful.
Take a good long look at me.

Dianna L. Grayer
2/8/2000

FYI—TO THE PRESIDENT AND HIS CABINET

To all LGBTs: This is your opportunity to come out and be counted. We must let our government know we exist and that we make up more than 10% of the population and that we come in all colors, religions, professions, and ages. We are diverse! Fill out the bottom portion and send it to the president. Make copies and give them to your friends. We want this to be the start of a movement. Come out come out wherever you are. We need to flood the mail going to the White House. You can e-mail them at president@whitehouse.gov

----

Date_____

President Bush
White House
Washington D. C.

Dear Mr. President,

I AM

Sexual orientation _____!

Race _____!

Female _____!

Male _____!

Profession _____!

Age _____!

Religion _____!

I want you to know I exist and I will not be changing any part of myself. I value all of myself. I want you and your cabinet to show LGBTs (lesbians, gays, bisexuals, and transgenders) respect. Give us the benefits and privileges you give to heterosexuals. We want to be safe and free in America too! From one of your citizens

I AM FREE

I am a free woman.
I am a free man.
I am Free.
I am not stuck in slavery.

I will hold my head high with confidence.
I will be proud of who I am.
I will be strong and courageous.
I will follow my truest path.
Because I am free.

I will be honest and trustworthy.
I will focus on my dreams and visions.
I will know that I am worthy of all the opportunities set before me.
I will know that I am capable of meeting all my goals.
Because I am free.

I will know that I am smart and able to become smarter.
I will know that I am capable of accomplishing great things.
I will know that if I don't do all the things
I know I'm capable of achieving
that it's because,
I didn't want to.
Not because I couldn't.

I am a free woman.
I am a free man.
I am Free.
I am not stuck in slavery.

Dianna L. Grayer
1/16/2000

WHO AM I, REALLY?

If I were totally honest with myself and others, who would I be?_____

_____

_____

_____

_____

_____

_____

_____

_____

_____

_____

_____

_____

_____

_____

_____

If I were totally believing and trusting in myself, what would I do?_____

_____

_____

_____

_____

_____

_____

_____

_____

_____

_____

_____

_____

_____

_____

_____

_____

If I were totally fearless of others and what they think of me, what would I say to them and how would I live my life?_____

_____

_____

_____

_____

_____

_____

_____

_____

_____

_____

_____

_____

_____

_____

If I were to eliminate my negative thoughts, feelings, and judgments about myself, how would I feel and how would my life change? (List all negative thoughts, feelings, and judgments to bring them into the light.)_____

_____

_____

_____

_____

_____

_____

_____

_____

_____

_____

_____

_____

_____

If I were honoring, respecting, loving, and accepting myself, how would my heart and soul feel?_____

_____

_____

_____

_____

_____

_____

_____

_____

_____

_____

_____

_____

_____

_____

_____

If I were living my life as a totally free person, I would be_____

_____

_____

_____

_____

_____

_____

_____

_____

_____

_____

_____

_____

_____

_____

_____

_____

CHALLENGE I

I challenge you to face your fears. Your fears prevent you from living fully. If you were to come out or to tell someone you've been wanting to tell but you would be too afraid, what frightens you?
List your fears:

I am afraid_____

I am afraid_____

I am afraid_____

I am afraid_____

I am afraid_____

I am afraid_____

I am afraid_____

What do you need to help you face your fears?
List the things that will help you:

I need_____

I need_____

I need_____

I need_____

I need_____

I need_____

Decide how you're going to get each of these needs met and make a step-by-step action plan for each one.

My plan:

Step 1 _____

_____

Step 2 _____

_____

Step 3 _____

_____

Step 4 _____

_____

Step 5 _____

_____

How did this process feel?_____

_____

_____

_____

_____

_____

_____

_____

_____

Repeat the steps on this page for all the fears you are faced with in your life.

STAND UP AND BE COUNTED

This exercise is to help you practice saying the words and feeling how it feels to come out and acknowledge a very important part of who you are. Look in the mirror and come out to yourself. Say the words out loud.
"I am_____ (fill in the blank with *gay, lesbian, bisexual* or *transgender*).

Repeat the phrase daily—as many times as it takes for you to become comfortable saying it and for you to be able to accept yourself. Begin with ten and move to one hundred. It would be helpful to keep a journal (writing down your feelings) of your progress.

Once you're comfortable with that phrase, then add "and I love myself and accept who I am." So it would look like this: "I am _____, and I love myself and accept who I am."

Repeat this phrase daily, as many times as it takes for you to become comfortable saying it and believing it. This stage should be easier. If not, start small and increase the number of times as you go. If you're convinced, others will be. Also, keeping a journal of your progress would be helpful.

Make a list of all the people you're going to tell once you're ready.

1._____   2._____
3._____   4._____
5._____   6._____
7._____   8._____
9._____   10._____

Explain your feelings as you think about coming out to these people.

_____

_____

_____

_____

_____

_____

_____

_____

Write down your fears immediately without thinking about them. Just listen to your body and write. Move this stuff out of yourself and into the light.

I'm afraid_____

I'm afraid_____

I'm afraid_____

I'm afraid_____

I'm afraid_____

I'm afraid_____

I'm afraid_____

Write immediately about how you feel after focusing on your fears and getting them out of your body._____

_____

_____

_____

_____

Repeat these steps as often as you need to, to understand yourself and your fears, and to move toward self-acceptance and freedom.

THE LIGHT

May the light of the flame be your inspiration
and your guide.
Let it remind you of the struggles of the
human race.
Let it remind you of the struggles people face
because of who they are or who they are not.
Let it remind you of the injustice and indignity
that people face every minute of the day.
Let it remind you of the pain, abuse and
victimization children and adults are subjected
to on a regular basis.
Let it remind you to speak out
 and fight against evil and wrongdoing.
Let it give you the strength and courage to be
 uncomfortable in order to push the issues.
Let it give to you whatever you need to
no longer tolerate unfairness and oppression.
Let it melt away your fears and silence.
And in the process,
you will see the light within yourself,
and know, that you are the light.
You are the light that can make a difference.

By Dianna L. Grayer
9/16/99

WHAT DO I HAVE TO DO?

We all have to contribute our part to gain our freedom as an LGBT person. So what's my part? _____

_____

_____

_____

_____

_____

_____

_____

What can I do to help myself? Refer to the topics in "Removing the Chains of Bondage" on pages 79 to 88, and list actions you can take to improve the way you express yourself in those categories.

1._____

2._____

3._____

4._____

5._____

6._____

7._____

8._____

9._____

10._____

When will I complete these goals?_____

What can I do to help others? Make a list of the things you can do—such as mentoring a child who is coming out, befriending an LGBT elder; speaking out in your home and to your family.

1._____

2._____

3._____

4._____

5._____

When will I complete these goals?_____

What can I do to help my community? Make a list of the things you can do—such as speaking to groups, educating parents and co-workers; supporting other LGBTs and their families in crises.

1._____

2._____

3._____

4._____

5._____

When will I complete these goals?_____

What can I do to help the world? Make a list of things you can do—such as fighting for the rights of LGBTs and other oppressed people around the world.

1._____

2._____

3._____

4._____

5._____

When will I complete these goals?_____

Use this space to express feelings you might be experiencing and to add other goals._____

CHALLENGE II

⚭❖⚭

Photocopy this page and fill it in every few weeks, or as serves you, to stay on track with meeting your needs and growing. You might want to keep a folder of the filled out pages, so that you can check from time to time to see if you are directing yourself towards your own goals.

⚭❖⚭

I challenge you to be happy and free. You can choose to live a happy and free life but there are certain changes you must make. You're the one who stops you.

List the changes you have to make:

I will change _____

I will change _____

I will change _____

I will change _____

I will change _____

What do you need to help you change?
List the things that will help you:

I need_____

I need_____

I need_____

I need_____

I need_____

Decide how you're going to get what you need and make a step-by-step action plan. My plan: is

Step 1 _____

_____

Step 2 _____

_____

Step 3 _____

_____

Step 4 _____

_____

Step 5 _____

_____

How did this process feel?_____

_____

_____

_____

_____

_____

_____

_____

_____

_____

_____

_____

_____

_____

_____

Repeat the steps on this page for all the changes you want to make in your life.

I PLEDGE ALLEGIANCE TO MYSELF

I am a capable human being who has the ability to become a productive and successful person in my community and the world.

I am powerful in my own right because I am a unique individual. There is no other like myself.

I have my own opinions, feelings, wants, and needs that distinguish who I am from others.

I have my own appearance, structure, style, likes, and dislikes that emphasize my individuality.

I am courageous in my need to be authentic. I will let my real self unfold and be seen by others.

I am lovable and equipped with the essentials needed for loving another and sustaining an intimate relationship.

I have values and morals that accentuate my uniqueness.

I have the knowledge and the strength to find the tools I need to deal with my stresses and mishaps within my life.

I am not perfect but I am able to learn from my mistakes. I will turn these lessons into future successes.

I have the strength and wisdom to make decisions and choices that will benefit me and my place in the world.

I have the ability to enjoy the pleasures that life brings me.

I pledge to be good to myself because I am important.

I will always love and respect myself and will always demand the same from others.

I pledge allegiance to my Self.

Dianna L. Grayer
2/1996

COLUMNS

My partner, Sheridan, and I wrote these following columns jointly. Our column is called "Living Proof" and can be found in *We the People*, a free paper serving the Sonoma County LGBT community. For the past two years we've dedicated some of our time, energy, and love in supporting the LGBT community in which we live. The columns are printed monthly and distributed the beginning of each month. We support, teach, and encourage our readers—always with the underlying theme of self-love, self-acceptance, and finding one's freedom. My hope is that these columns will do the same for you. Share them with your friends and family. Invite a group over, and use them to create conversation and a lively discussion. This is a way for you to hear what your friends and family think and feel about the different topics. Happy Learning!

(If you're interested in receiving future columns, contact *We the People* at WTP, Att: Subscriptions, P.O. Box 12126, Santa Rosa, CA 95406, and join the mailing list.)

December 2000

CREATING FAMILY

As a result of our own childhood experiences of not having our emotional needs met, we wanted to create our own family. But first we had to define what family meant to us. Is it only the group you are born into? Is it only defined by blood relatives? We refused to settle for what we were born into dealing only with negative, unaccepting family members and the corresponding tension. We believe that in a family, the key is that one feels nurtured, connected, heard, accepted, loved, and supported. As we all know, many gay, lesbian, bisexual, and trans-gendered people have not experienced this acceptance in their biological families. Either the tension was too much to bear or we were rejected altogether. In our biological families we weren't rejected, however, neither were we celebrated.

When we set out to create our own family, we wanted supportive people around us and children living with us, but how were we going to bring friends

109

and children into our lives? Amazingly, once we knew what we wanted, and put it out in the universe, we began to connect with others who wanted the same thing. Friends came into our lives, with and without children, gay, and straight. We all felt free to be who we were with each other. What a relief!

Then there was the subject of having children. We both wanted children but neither of us wanted to become pregnant. We explored many options and decided that our best choice was foster care. Biological kids were pretty much out of the question, as we would have wanted the sperm donor to be a biological family member, and no men were up for the challenge (neither were we!). Adoption just didn't feel right: it somehow would limit the number of children we could help. We knew there were many kids from broken families in need, both of homes and of people to care for them. Foster care called out to us. We wanted to show children a new way of being in the world. We would be loving and accepting parents, teach our foster children to love and to accept themselves; and, through their own journey, we would help them to realize that they didn't have to mirror their backgrounds, that they had

choices in how they wanted to be in the world. Foster care, moreover, was a gift both to them, and to us – not to mention to society. To us, being a Lesbian couple was of little consequence when applying to be foster parents: either social workers were going to place kids with us or they were not—while 15 years and 20 kids later speak for themselves.

As foster parents we were able to choose the child we wanted placed in our home. We considered age, race, personality, sexual orientation, interests, background and personal issues, and biological family involvement. Once the kids moved in, it was about getting to know each other and building a trusting relationship. It was a difficult time for these children missed their biological families. Weekly family meetings were a helpful format that allowed them to open up and share their feelings. They learned to express themselves, and, as importantly, they learned to listen to the self expression of others. Presently, we have three foster daughters living with us, ages 13, 12, and 9. Creating this kind of family was the answer to years of our feeling separate from those families who had given us birth. As well as these children, we've been able to welcome other positive and loving friends with whom to share our lives. We are worthy people and deserve to be celebrated. You, too, can create the family you want. You need not settle for less. We are living proof.

Feb 2001

IN HONOR OF OUR FRIEND

We're all familiar with the words, "Be all that you can be." Yes, the famous military slogan. It is a complete lie. You can't be all that you can be in the military if you can't be open about your sexual orientation. How can a person be truly her/his best? If we can't be free to be all of what we are, we will NEVER BE OUR BEST.

Our friend served for over twenty years in a branch of the military, received top honors, and eventually made her way up the ranks to the top. She dedicated her life to the military, hoping to retire in a couple of years and live on her pension. Unfortunately our friend died before her retirement. She died in the military's closet. Be all that you can be but we don't want to know you. Be all that you can be but you can't be yourself. Our friend served for so many years. The military put her to rest not knowing who she really was, or the depth of pain the closet caused her.

Our friend left behind her partner of twenty years, who traveled with her from station to station around the country, and waited for her when she was stationed abroad. The two of them grew up together, loving and caring for each other, but had to be quiet about it. They were only friends and roommates to the people who say, "Come, be all that you can be." Our hearts go out to her partner, also our friend, who had to remain in the closet even after her death. She had to plan the funeral in secret, telling her partner's wishes to the blood sister, while the blood sister and the military planned the funeral in the open. She was in the shadows, watching, not really existing. During the flag ceremony, she wasn't even acknowledged, as two flags were given to two different biological family members.

Unfortunately, logistics prevented us from attending her funeral to say our good-byes, however we couldn't imagine seeing all those uniforms and not want to scream. Instead, we stayed home and wrote this article and lit candles, remembering our wonderful times together and the loss we feel not having her in our lives.

She was such a sweet, loving, generous, and good person. She had a lovely soul and spirit. She was always striving to be her best, learning and growing, even with so much pressure not to be herself. She just grinned and beared it as the saying goes. We admired her dearly and were deeply saddened by the load she was carrying. She was so young. Her life was just beginning. She told us soon after she was diagnosed with cancer that it was a wake up call. She had remembered telling herself every morning she went to work to serve her country, "I'm killing myself." She worked so hard to prove to the military that she was okay, that she was worthy of being completely acknowledged for who she was. The terrible tragedy is that she died trying to be the best that she could be, but she could never be her best because she couldn't be herself.

When you can't be yourself, you can't completely live. Parts of you die, and then all of your parts die. Our hearts are full of many emotions from sadness to rage. It's upsetting to know that so many of us, by standing in the closet, allow others to control our lives. What is better, to live and die a lie, or to live and die free?

In honor of our friend, we light a candle for all our sisters and brothers serving in the military, for those who can't be all that they can be. Please join us. Come out where ever you are. You deserve to live free, and in honor of yourself. Be free before you die. COOBODAY (Grant strength, courage and guidance.)

March 2001

BEATING FEAR

So often people want to do something in their lives, but fear gets in their way. Fear becomes so powerful that it stops them from taking the first step. It could be fear of how it will turn out, fear of losing what you have, fear of the stress that may result, or the fear of how others might react. Fear comes from the place of the unknown -or known if you've experienced a traumatic event. One's mind takes over and gets trapped in *What If*.

What If is how we keep ourselves stuck. We talk ourselves out of things. We become irrational. There's a voice that says we can't, no matter what the reality is.

Take *our* fears (those of Dianna and Sheridan) as examples:

Dianna: "As a kid, my fear of water was so bad that I used to run out of the bathroom when I flushed the toilet, thinking the water would drown me. What if I couldn't breathe?

As an adult, I stayed far away from pools. I realized that my fear blocked me from having fun in the water, as I watched so many people enjoying themselves. I took it upon myself to face my fear and taught myself how to swim.

"Another fear, public speaking, was unavoidable. Everywhere I went, in school and in every job, I had to speak publicly. What if my words didn't come out right? What if I wasn't understood? I would obsess, lose sleep, and on the day of the event, I would disassociate: my body would shake, and I couldn't eat.

"It was extreme. I even turned down coaching jobs, speaking engagements, and social events. I loved coaching and teaching, but my fear stopped me from these experiences. With work and determination, I pushed myself to overcome my fear of public speaking. As a result I'm doing the things I wanted to do and knew I was capable of doing."

Sheridan: "When I knew a confrontation was coming up, my heart rate increased, I started hyperventilating, and my stomach tightened. What if they yelled at me? I never thought I could hold my own. But as I grew more secure, I realized I didn't have to lose myself. I could keep who I was, explain my point of view, and move on.

"Another fear was coming out to my students. It was so hard to be in the closet when kids made anti-gay jokes and homophobic remarks. What if my students didn't like me when they found out I was gay? Staying in the closet however, chipped away at my self-worth and prevented me from being the teacher I knew I could be. By building my self-confidence, and with a lot of reflection—together with Dianna's support and encouragement—I came out to my students, and I've never looked back."

Take a moment to think about your fears. What are your What If's? Imagine your life without them. What would you be doing, and how would you be feeling?

So many people go through life not fully living due to their fears. There came a time when we had to stop letting our fears control us. You can do the same. Make your goal to move through your fears by challenging yourself to face them. In overcoming your fears you have to take the first step, acknowledging them to yourself.

The next step is acknowledging them to someone else. Bring your fears out of the closet and into the light so that they can be fully examined. Confront your What If's. Then make a step-by-step plan to overcome them. Practice by putting yourself in those uncomfortable situations and follow your healing by keeping a journal of your concerns, attempts, processes, and accomplishments.

Facing fears is a liberating experience. Don't let your fears stop you from living your life to its fullest. Be kind to yourself and know that you can beat the fear.

April 2001

HOW CAN WE COUNT OURSELVES IF WE DON'T KNOW WHO WE ARE ?

One Saturday morning, while shopping at our local Home Depot, we believe we saw a Lesbian at every turn —and gay men in the store, too. It was amazing and comforting. However, the disappointing part of it was that as we tried to make eye contact to pass a friendly knowing smile, no one returned the gesture. As we walked by each brother or sister, our likeness was invisible. Why is it that gay people don't acknowledge each other in public?

It's a much different experience when Di sees another Black person. Di and the other Black person usually acknowledge each other with a smile, and a, "How are you doin'?" [**Sheridan** speaking] "For twenty-three years I have been observing this unspoken understanding, this code. At first I felt left out, because I wasn't included in their hellos. But now I understand. It doesn't have anything to do with me. It has to do with Di's history, and the history of oppression. It doesn't matter that they don't know each other. It's pretty wonderful." [**Dianna** speaking] "There are so few Blacks in Marin and Sonoma, so it's great to see someone like me. There's a commonality and a mutual understanding when we're passing each other. We nod and say hello. It's nice."

So why is it that gay folks don't acknowledge each other in public? Is it shyness? Is it the fear of coming out? Is it uncomfortable wondering if someone may or may not be gay, and how do we know, so why even try to make contact? Is it the fear that if you smile at someone s/he might think you are trying to pick him or her up? Or is it that we are so numerous we don't have to take the time to say hello? Are we — Sheridan and Dianna—the only ones that have this experience? We have no clue as to what is going on inside everyone's head, but we have a question for you: How are we going to build community if we don't acknowledge our gayness to each other? This phenomena isn't isolated to Home Depot. It's the same in any public place, in any town, whether it be shopping for groceries or seeing a movie. How can we expect the world to acknowledge us if we can't acknowledge each other?

We want to be counted, but we don't let ourselves come out to be counted. The research says that 10% of the population is gay. Maybe it's more than 10%. How do researchers know if we don't allow ourselves be seen? The next time you go shopping or to a public place where there's lots of people, notice who's around. Count the number of sisters and brothers you see and notice how many notice you. Pay attention to how you feel in the moment.

The questions are many: What can we do to support each other? How can we help each other feel safe enough to come out? How can we make coming out a goal for inner peace and self-actualization? How can we acknowledge each other in our community? How can we show the world that we may represent more than 10 percent?

We feel strongly that the more we stay secluded and in the closet, the more we are divided both as a community and as a people. Straight people will continue to be upfront and in control. **WE MUST STAND STRONG**, acknowledge each other and come together. Think about this: If we are stronger as a unit, we will be better equipped to fight against those who are disapproving, unaccepting, and determined to break us down.

Let us know if you have an idea of how to acknowledge each other when we're out and about in public. But in the meantime, here's our idea: Let us begin by a simple action. Let us begin by smiling that smile. Let us begin by having the light shine in our eyes. And let us begin by saying, "Hello." It can happen. We are living proof. We'll smile back.

May 2001

YOU ARE YOUR BEST RESOURCE

Spring is here! It is bright, cheerful, warm and colorful. It's a breath of fresh air, and everything comes alive. People have traditionally used springtime as a time to clean up the clutter they have collected throughout the year. It is a time when people get rid of unwanted stuff in and outside their homes. People focus on the garden and flower beds, removing all the weeds and extra growth from the winter. They're able to plant new seeds and see them grow— whether it be fruit, vegetables or flowers. Springtime is a fresh start after a dark and wet winter. It is a time for change.

We would like to add to the tradition of spring cleaning. Using this metaphor we would like to make of this time a tradition to remove the clutter and deadness from the inside. One can start anew by planting seeds for growth, change and the healing of the human spirit—an endeavor that will also allow the bulbs that have been dormant due to clutter and neglect to come alive.

It is amazing to discover the many problems people deal with on a daily basis. The unfortunate and very sad thing about this discovery is that many people seem to feel helpless, thinking they have no way out of their situation. They just settle in and accept where they are; and, while superficially this

acceptance might appear to get them by, their attitude, behavior and mood show otherwise.

If people would interpret spring cleaning to also mean cleaning up their spirit, they might live happier, healthier lives, since they would be paying attention to themselves— Internally shifting this energy to make their lives better and their souls lighter, enhancing everything they touch. They would see the springtime within *and* without.

Perhaps you're wondering how to get started. We suggest you do as you normally would when you clean out your home and garden. Follow the same rules and process. However, in your home and garden, you can see what needs to be changed or discarded, unlike inside yourself. Therefore, it would be advantageous for you first to spend time reflecting upon the past year. How happy were you? Were you as productive as you wanted to be? What burdens were you carrying?

Perhaps you have been sad, or there is a relationship issue you need to resolve. Maybe your health or self-esteem are not where you want them to be. All these things can change if you attend to yourself as you would attend to your garden and home.

Take a close look at what you want to change and remove the things that are dead, damaged, not used, or not working. Make a list so it will be there to remind you. Prioritize the things that were most difficult for you, things that stopped you from growing, changing and healing, things that blocked your happiness, freedom and, ultimately, your inner peace.

Once you compile your list it is time for you to get busy. You are ready to experience springtime and the rest of your life as you never have before. You're ready to make yourself blossom into the beautiful, deserving flower that you are. Let the beauty from within shine as brightly as the new flowers of spring.

Take the first task on your list and make it right, the way that is best for you. Then move to the next. Take one step at a time in making your life the way you want it to be. You have the #1 tool you need—which is yourself.

You know the changes you need to make. You have what it takes to create both within yourself and around you the beauty, brightness, cheer and color of springtime. Don't settle for a life of winters when you can have a life full of springtimes. It

can be done. We are living proof. Happy growing!

June 2001

SEEING OUR PARENTS, SEEING OURSELVES

As May is past and June is here, many people—in the midst of the parental holidays—take the time to reflect about their parents. As LGBTQ people, many of us have had hurtful things happen to us, and the hurt might even be continuing today. Sometimes people hold on to that hurt.

We—Dianna and Sheridan— believe that resentment and anger block peace and happiness. So, how does one go about ridding oneself of these feelings that drain and stain? How does one go about the cleansing that has to take place before the calm of inner peace can exist? Sometimes it might be journaling, therapy, listening to healing music, writing that letter to your mom or dad that you never send, talking with friends, talking with siblings, seeing your parent inside you as you parent your children—and perhaps, for some of us, visiting with our parents. That's what did it for Sheridan.

Sheridan: I began my coming out process when I was 17, and met

Di when I was 21. I didn't tell my parents about our relationship for 7 years. It was ten years later before we received our first anniversary card from my mom.

Now, twenty-three-and-a-half years later, tension between my family members and me still exists. I have a lot to be resentful about. I know deep in my heart that, if I were with a man, I would have a wonderful relationship with my sisters and parents. However, I made the choice to be honest about who I am, and, with lots of personal reflection, made the choice to let go of my family's issues.

This April I visited my parents in Florida and made peace within myself. My dad had had open heart surgery four months prior, and I went to help my mom. For the first time I saw them as vulnerable people like the rest of us, and my anger and resentment melted away. As I flew home four days later, my soul felt rested. I was calm. I felt a peace inside that remains unexplainable. I still carry that peace within me now.

Dianna: Even though I was unhappy most of my childhood, I chose not to let anger and resentment fill me. As a child, I like to think that I had an unusual strength and wisdom. I made a promise to myself that I wanted to live with peace within and around me, and that I wasn't going to let anyone, even my parents, be an obstacle. I realized that my parents would never be able to nurture me the way I needed them to. It just wasn't their style, and they weren't willing to learn. So I detached, knowing we are different individuals and that I didn't have to let their stuff be my stuff.

This was peace, representing an understanding both of my parents and myself. I healed my hurt and pain by re-parenting myself. I gave my inner child what my parents couldn't give me. With this peace, I am now able lovingly to assist my mother, who is disabled from a stroke. My father passed away years ago.

There are often family gatherings honoring mothers and fathers, and these gatherings are opportunities to acknowledge the feelings you are harboring. Understand them. Confront the ones you can; let go of the ones you can't; and heal the ones that hurt. Remember that ultimately how we deal with issues involving ourselves and our parents is a choice. We don't necessarily have to confront those issues that block our peace and happiness. See your parents separately from yourself. Free yourself. You can do it. We are living proof.

July 2001
TRUE FREEDOM

July is here. It's a time to acknowledge our independence and freedom. Living in a free country is truly a blessing, but when we look within our country we know there are many people who aren't really free. Who knows if people will ever have true freedom? But think about this: What about obtaining true freedom from within?

What does having true freedom mean to you? Do you feel free at home, at your job, with family, in relationships, within your community and within yourself? We, Dianna and Sheridan, like to look at true freedom as having personal power. Personal power is taking control of your life and living your life freely. It's an assertive outpouring of who you truly are and what you truly believe. Personal power is honoring yourself, doing what's best no matter what anyone says or thinks, and it's loving yourself. If you hear a demeaning joke, what do you do—laugh to fit in; stand up and say something; stay silent and sacrifice your own

integrity? Do you allow people to know who you really are?

Dianna: As a therapist especially, but also with friends and family, I observe many people who lack personal power. They feel unhappy and trapped because they don't have control of their lives. They feel controlled by others, hearing others' voices over their own. They sacrifice their wants and needs for others. Who they are gets lost, and their sense of self is gone. This lack of personal power doesn't discriminate. I see it in children, adults and culturally diverse populations. A very important goal of mine has always been—no matter what arena—to help people achieve true freedom, freedom within. I ask the questions that haven't been asked, and they come up with the answers that they've been avoiding. Total honesty in every aspect of one's life is true personal power.

Sheridan: As a teacher I see teenagers constantly struggling trying to figure out who they should be—themselves or their friends. Peer pressure is huge and many of my students want to fit in at any risk. They make poor decisions and feel bad, but not bad enough to change. They can't trust themselves to do the right thing. Being liked and accepted by their peers takes priority, and facing their parents and themselves is far less important. It takes a strong individual to honor her/himself first. Obtaining personal power is my focus in helping at-risk youths.

We, Dianna and Sheridan, are always honoring ourselves and encouraging others to honor themselves. Honoring yourself symbolizes self-acceptance and self-love for who you are. This is your ticket to true freedom. Many people get stuck here and ask how to become unstuck. Here are some ways that have helped us:

Be self-aware and notice what bothers you and why. Say what you think and feel. Be honest. Protect yourself. Don't let others mistreat you. Don't do things you don't want to do just to avoid disappointing others. Make "no" mean "no" and "yes" mean "yes." Demand respect. Demand a balanced relationship. Always be good to your inner child. Do things that bring you joy. Laugh, cry, understand yourself. Be healthy. Believe in yourself. Trust yourself. And always count your blessings.

Personal power is a goal that everyone must strive to achieve if we want to be truly free. We are all worthy and valuable people and have that

right. So aim for true freedom by honoring yourself. Exert your personal power and see yourself unfold before your own eyes. It can be done. We are living proof.

August 2001

GET OUT OF YOUR COMFORT ZONE

Why do confrontations have to be so hard? Confrontation, as stated by Webster's, is "a meeting expressed face to face," but when people think about the act of confrontation, the thought immediately evokes anxiety.

Take a moment to think about all of the times you've wanted to confront someone, but you didn't. What stopped you, and how did you feel after making the decision not to? After all the times you didn't express your feelings, did you let things build up until you exploded or acted out in other ways? Did you crawl under a rock and disappear? Were you afraid of how another would respond to you, fearful that s/he would lash out in anger or be disappointed, hurt, or even discount what you had to say? Or, if you did confront someone, did you feel bad about yourself because you told the truth and hurt someone's feelings or made them angry? We can't control how others take our messages, but we owe it to ourselves to say what is real for us.

Sheridan: Confrontation has always been a struggle for me. Fortunately, I have a partner who won't let me get away with being silent, and during our remodeling work recently, she again pushed me out of my comfort zone of passivity and forced me out from under my rock—for I was no longer able to ignore this problem.

I remembered something a therapist said to me regarding the event: "It's not what I want to say, it's what I want him (the contractor) to know. I can't control what he feels, but I can say what I need to say, kindly." Those were very freeing words to me, and since then I have voiced my concerns more readily and with more confidence. As uncomfortable as this is, I know it's good for me because I feel stronger, more free, relieved and empowered whenever I speak what's real for me.

Dianna: In my younger years I was shy and didn't say much. However, when things bothered me I paid attention. The gnawing in my gut was my body telling me something was wrong. I eventually began to respond to my feelings by sharing them. It was a scary thing though, because

I was raised in a way in which confrontation meant loud arguing, cursing, and physical violence. I decided that I didn't have to communicate that way, that I could confront people with seriousness, but respectfully.

I'm now known for my honesty and directness. The best way to be is straight-up, clear, and to the point. However, many people don't know how to be this way. Confrontation doesn't have to be a negative thing. It's stating what is. In my experience people avoid saying what is their truth to protect themselves and others.

I believe you can't take care of other's feelings; that's their job. When you ignore the gnawing sensation, you sell yourself short. You've cheated yourself and the person involved, because it could have been, for both of you, an experience of learning and of growth.

Confrontation is necessary. If you don't confront others you're saying you're not important, that what the person is doing is okay. Pay attention at all the times that you don't ignore the gnawing in your stomach. Imaginatively practice difficult conversations or awkward work situations. Use a tape recorder and/or video camera. Find a practice buddy. Replay the scenes and try a different way. Keep a journal. Speak to your fears and find someone to listen. Your voice is dying to get out, and when you finally let it out, you will be stronger, wiser and more connected to yourself. You can do it. We're living proof.

September 2001

TIME IS FLYING

Unbelievable, but it's September already. Summer has come and gone. The kids are back in school, and the shopping frenzy for the holidays is headed right for us. Just like that—another summer has rolled by.

The interesting question is, how much of it do you remember? What parts were important, joyous, unproductive? What parts were spent on personal growth and connection with yourself?

Our lives are mostly built on being busy. Some people feel when they are busy that they are productive and that makes them okay. Others feel good about themselves when they are surrounded by material things and never stop to reflect about what they might be losing by getting all that "stuff."

However, keeping busy prevents you from paying attention and connecting to yourself, which only causes problems down the way, emotionally and physically. In actuality, another summer has passed by, and, after some reflection, you might realize you have been stuck in the frenzy, letting time fly by.

Dianna: In my experience counseling people, it's clear that many are struggling, trapped in the frenzy of "busyness," trying to keep up with others. To every client that comes to see me, I emphasize the art of slowing down. They're moving too fast to notice themselves, as if time were running out. Many of them are on paths that aren't truly their own because they haven't taken the time to reflect upon their true path, only the path that others have paved for them. I remember an exercise one of my professors in graduate school had the class participate in. It was to eat a banana very slowly, noticing the texture, how it felt in our mouths, on our teeth and tongue. It was amazing that something so simple impacted my life forever. I had never paid that much attention to eating a banana.

For the first time I felt the texture, the thickness forced in between my teeth, the way the banana changed from dry to wet as I chewed and swallowed. This is how I try to live life, being present and aware of whatever I'm doing, exploring and reflecting along the way, and when I realize I'm moving too quickly, I take a deep breath and think about the banana—which immediately slows me down.

Sheridan: Last year I was in go mode. Living with Di was a constant reminder to slow down, but at times I forgot and had to pay the price—which manifested in irritability. It was difficult because I had so much on my plate, i.e., teaching full-time, going through a major remodel, and raising four foster daughters. I know and feel the value of slowing down and have chosen to teach part-time this school year. I will focus my energy on slowing down and experiencing the fullness of everything I do because my time *is* my experience. I have listened to myself and I am taking care of myself. I am choosing to eat my banana another way, instead of inhaling it and complaining that I have a stomach ache.

Time is always moving, sometimes faster than we would like. However, it's important to slow down and take the time to notice yourself and what you're doing. Remember, it's your time and you get to choose how you want to use it. Your time can fly by and be gone, or you can slow

down and *be* your time. Eat your banana slowly. It can be done. We are living proof.

January 2002

IS REJECTION ALWAYS A BAD THING?

We hope your new year will be full of introspection. So let's start with this thought: Is rejection always a bad thing? When most people think of the word rejection, it's usually something that's very hurtful. LGBT's know rejection on both a global level and on an individual one. People of color know rejection as well. Rejection is part of our fabric. We know that it can be devastating to have a person who is madly in love with another rejected because the feeling isn't mutual, a person in the same firm for years watching everyone else being promoted, or an actor not getting the lead in a play.

However, it seems that we human beings hold rejection too high. We view rejection as denial of something that we wanted. This means we cause pain to ourselves. Imagine if we all changed our thinking about the act of being rejected to a more positive light. We would naturally change our reactions, both emotional and physical. This way we would control our feelings of rejection. We [Dianna and Sheridan] see it as self-value and inner strength. We believe rejection is not always a bad thing but an opportunity for a person to follow her/his true path.

Dianna: I was rejected many times around jobs, friendships and by publishers. When I look back, I didn't want those jobs anyway, why would I want to be friends with people who didn't see my beauty, and I always had faith and believed that the right publisher would accept my book. And if people don't like me because I'm Black and/or Lesbian that's about them, not me.

Sheridan: Friends and family have rejected me also. Who knows why friends just all of a sudden never returned calls or made up excuses not to see me? Many of my family members don't acknowledge my relationship with Dianna and the tension over the years has been physically unsettling. I can't go on worrying about something that's out of my control. I have to know and believe I am good and capable of creating a happy and healthy life for myself.

Just recently our thoughts and feelings about rejection have been validated. [Dianna] Early in September, I knew it was close to basketball season and started to call my teammates of three years.

We discovered our team had formed a team without us. For whatever the reason, I was told the team voted not to include us and not to call us to let us know. Instead of feeling bad, I was energized. I love basketball and I was going to play. I called and recruited players. I immediately got a sponsor who paid our fees and bought T-shirts. We came together as a team and are undefeated going into the playoffs. We're having the best time and often think about sending my old team a thank you note.

This is an example of valuing oneself and believing you deserve better. Why would a person want to be with people who don't want to be with them? It's important to look back at the times you were devastated due to rejection. Did you make yourself the bad person? Perhaps it wasn't the place for you and the right place is coming. Try to change your thinking so you can continue forward on your journey to a place where you truly want to be. Remember, you deserve to be where you are wanted and accepted, and if you don't have that, go find it. It can be done. We are living proof.

April 2002

COMMUNICATING IS LIKE DANCING

Dianna: Take a moment and think about your upbringing and how you were raised to communicate your feelings. Did your parent(s) actually sit you down and demonstrate the one, two, three's of communication like they might have with tying your shoes or riding your bike? My guess is no. Communicating is like dancing with another person. If your steps are not together, there will be problems.

Communication is so important in our day-to-day existence that it should have been taken more seriously when we were young. Especially because we all grow up and venture into relationships with others. The way my family communicated anger was by yelling and hitting. I was taught to stifle my thoughts and feelings and was raised with the philosophy that children should be seen, not heard. Anger in Sher's family was communicated by silence. Because of our different experiences, we were definitely off beat and stepped on each other's toes. Now add our different cultural backgrounds, and there is a recipe for communication breakdown! It took years for Sher and me to learn the new steps to communication, and it was a definite struggle. But we were determined to learn the one, two, three's to secure our relationship.

I'm able to see the seriousness of peoples' inability to communicate honestly, especially with my clients. For whatever reason, they can't express their opinions and desires with others. When I give my couples an assignment to spend roughly ten minutes a day together talking about something personal, so often I get blank stares. They don't know the dance steps.

When two people get together and make a com-mitment, they're embarking on an adventure of a lifetime. Often these people haven't individuated yet, perhaps because they still follow parental and/or societal voices, doubting their own voices. (Take closeted gays, for example.) This self-doubt is camouflaged in habits such as perfectionism, blaming, anger, defensiveness, stubbornness, pas-sivity, depression, illness, and addiction. All of these expressions will cause problems in a relationship, and because both partners haven't been taught the steps to honest communication, problems are inevitable.

When I see couples who are having communication problems, I use the metaphor of dance. They need to learn a new dance, one free of the constant stepping and tripping on each other's feet. They need to learn a new way of communicating which involves saying their truth, trusting that their feelings are important, listening without interrupting, paraphrasing, compromising, and negotiating. These are the new steps to the dance, and they start with honoring and valuing yourself and your partner. With hard work and dedication to the process, couples learn to understand the dynamics in the relationship (oh, this is what's happening...) and their own personal contributions to those dynamics (and this is my part...). Each partner takes responsibility and ownership of making the relationship work. They learn the new dance steps and move the relationship to a more peaceful and satisfying place.

Learning to communicate with Sher and others has been an important journey toward my personal and professional growth. I know what it takes to change dysfunctional and unproductive ways of communication. If you are having communication problems with your partner, make the commitment to change. Begin your journey and learn your new dance. If you need help, seek a professional. You deserve to dance smoothly and joyfully. Sher and I are always practicing our steps. It can be done. We are living proof.

May 2002

FIND YOUR BALANCE

Finding true balance is a lifelong struggle for many people. We (Dianna and Sheridan) are convinced that only through balance will we be able to attain true peace. By true peace, we mean internal peace; finding a job that is fulfilling, being able to pay bills without guilt or anxiety, experiencing good health, finding time to be involved in personal growth experiences, being emotionally available to your kids, your partner, your colleagues, your friends. How is balance attainable? You have to be able to set limits in your life. You have to know when to say okay, and when to say no without guilt. Otherwise you'll drown.

Sheridan: Something I've learned over the years is to give myself time to be alone and do something I enjoy. Sure, I could think of it as taking away from the family. Or I can think of it as giving to myself so that I will have more to give my family. I am no good to anyone if I am full of resentment and fatigue. So I drum. And I take yoga. Drumming and yoga bring balance to my tipped scale of service; I serve my foster kids, my students, my administration, my partner, my pets, and the bill collectors. I have to take some of the time for me. I have to. My soul would die if I didn't. That means I have to say no often. It means I work part-time. I have learned to say no to the outside world and yes to Sheridan.

Dianna: I am truly blessed by the balance I have created in my life. I give, I receive, play, pray, create, and appreciate. I am a happier and freer person as a result of the balance I've created. Because of my ability to balance my life and know its value, I am able to help others find balance in theirs. Most often it's just a matter of switching the focus from outward to inward. So when you feel out of sorts, take the time to pay attention to where most of your energy is going, and make a change.

Too many people are suffocating and they don't know why. They're overwhelmed, tired, and unhappy and don't have the tools to get in balance. Why do we let ourselves get out of balance? When did it happen?

We lost touch with ourselves, when we are trying to please and take care of others, or when we try to do too much. This is when people feel their lives are out of control. Problems occur. They get sick, they're impatient, they're angry and they don't know how to stop.

Are you one of these people? If you feel overwhelmed at the moment, make a list and write down everything that you have to do on the left side of the page. Put a 1 by the most important things you do. Take all the 1's and put them into 2 columns. Label one column, "For Others." Label the other column, "For Me." How many of your 1's are for others? How many of them are for yourself? Each column should have nearly the same amount. You should have balance in that list of your most important things to do, because you're most important. If you keep giving to others without filling yourself up, you will have little left to give. Think of a car. When it is out of gas, it gets filled up or it dies. It can't just keep going and going without refueling. Neither can you.

What fills you up? What brings you back into balance? You owe it to yourself to find your balance. It can be done. We are living proof.

June 2002

HAVE A HEART

When June arrives it reminds us of freedom parades held around the world. What a beautiful thing it is to be out on a lovely day celebrating our freedom and our existence with others. However, there are many LGBT's who are unable to join in the celebration because they are fearful of the consequences of being dis-covered. It is for these people we are writing this month.

We remember the line that says it all, "HAVE A HEART!" We want to open our hearts to our sisters and brothers who can't be with us as we celebrate being out of the closet. We know what a gift it is to be free, not to be stuck in a place we don't want to be. For those of you who are out of the closet, do you remember what it was like when you were in? We do. It was like accepting a jail sentence even though we hadn't committed any wrongdoing. We had to censor what we said, omitting things that people might question. Or we'd get that nervous feeling in our stomachs when a gay issue came into conversation. We created our own prison based on fear.

Dianna: I was mostly in the closet with my family, and with others I do admit to censoring my speech. As I grew into me, I stopped doing that. Now, my life's work is about transitioning a person from a place of bondage to a place of freedom. Since June is here I've found myself having a heavy heart for those LGBT's who have settled for the life of invisibility. Coming out is a difficult journey, however, the outcome is freedom. You will know when it is time to transition. In the meantime, I wish you well. Always know that you deserve freedom.

Sheridan: I know the life of being in the closet. My fears imprisoned me. What if anyone found out, especially my students? I knew they would laugh at me and I wasn't ready for that. With lots of inner-work and self-acceptance, I'm free now. I'm out to my students and I'm able to discuss homophobia. Because of my actions, my school is a better and safer place for my students and myself.

To those who are in the closet, we feel your struggle. Know that others see your sacrifice. Always be kind and loving toward yourself. Don't let those who don't understand you break your spirit. May your higher power watch over you and give you the strength and courage to find your way to experience your freedom—the freedom that is rightfully yours. Know that some day you will be able to celebrate your freedom.

For all of us who are able to be free from the life of living in the closet, take a moment and be thankful. Give thanks and pray for all our sisters and brothers who are unable to walk the free life with us. And if you're attending a freedom day parade, stand proud and shout with your fist high above your head, "To my sisters and brothers who can't be here today!"

Remember, all of us have struggles, whether in the closet or out. We're all trying to find our way. So when you see someone struggling, offer a kind word or a helping hand. Remember to have a heart, knowing that we all get places at different times. With warmth in our hearts, we celebrate all of our LGBT comrades around the world. You can celebrate them, too. It can be done. With love in our hearts, we are living proof.

July 2002

RECEIVING IS PART OF SELF-CARE

Recently we were invited to join other foster/adopt parents on a retreat where the focus was Better Self Care for Better Foster Care. We had facilitators teach us how to stretch, meditate, and take care of our backs; our meals were prepared, and we were able to network with each other, vent, rejuvenate, and receive.

Receiving is difficult for most people. Some deny their needs altogether, and others don't feel worthy enough of having their needs met and are too shy to ask. Although the parents at this retreat were exhausted, it became clear that most of them had a difficult time asking to have their needs met. As they shared their stories and exhausting daily routines, it was hard for them to receive those precious hours for themselves.

Self-care is essential for two reasons. One is if we don't take care of ourselves, we feel dissatisfied and unhappy. The other is we won't be able to care for others without building resentment.

As the retreat continued, we heard how parents worked non-stop and then crashed. They gave and gave but weren't replenishing themselves by receiving from others. We all need to be able to receive. If we don't allow ourselves to receive, we become resentful and lose our glow. Do you give and give and give until you crash? Have you lost your glow?

Dianna: Years ago Sher and I vowed to take better care of ourselves emotionally, physically, mentally, and spiritually. This was an important journey for me. It was hard for me to receive in my younger years because I was big tough Di and I didn't need anyone. As I grew older, I learned that I didn't have to carry my load alone. As I healed my childhood wounds, I learned to ask for what I needed. Guess what? I got it. I feel blessed to be on the path of self-care. It is wonderful not to carry the extra load. I am nurtured in ways I've only dreamed about. I don't have to be strong 24/7 and my soul can feel the difference.

Sheridan: I've had to learn to ask for what I need. But it's one thing to ask, yet another to allow. I've had to allow others to do for me as I do for them. It's amazing how good I feel receiving what I give. I was raised to think it was selfish. It's been a long lesson to really believe that I deserve to receive the care that I so freely give to others.

It's important to give yourself permission to receive. Parents, ask someone to watch your kids for a few hours. Your kids will be fine. Workaholics,

slow down and stop avoiding your needs. Caregivers, let your partners or friends care for you. For all of you who are always doing for others, stop working on empty. Let someone fill you up by giving to you. You will definitely reap the benefits. You will feel it in your body, in your relationship and in your soul.

Start today. What needs of yours have you been neglecting? Is it really hard for you to ask for things and to receive from others? Write your concerns down and then share them with someone. Let your loved ones, including your children, know what your needs are. It's not selfish. You are worthy, and you're being a good role model for your children and those around you. It's your time to be the recipient of someone else's energy. Go ahead. Let your wall down. You can do it. We're living proof.

August 2002

LEARNING THE COUPLE DANCE

When speaking to other couples about their trials and tribulations, we came up with a metaphor: Couples are learning to dance with each other. It's a process every couple goes through, and putting a picture to the process makes it easier to understand. You are two different people from two different worlds coming together to make a relationship harmonious. Sometimes your toes get stepped on, sometimes you step on hers. Sometimes you hold him at the waist, sometimes he holds you, and sometimes you don't know who's supposed to hold whom!

Granted, you may have some commonalities that were exciting in the beginning of your relationship. But once the relationship has moved forward, you begin to see more clearly how different the two of you really are. Your money management or work ethic might be different. Your organization and housekeeping skills may be completely opposite, but the one thing that is solid is that you both care about each other. So when things get tough, try hard to come back to this place to ground yourselves in the love you share.

Many relationships end because people don't want to work things out. Each partner leaves and moves on to another relationship, always looking for that perfect someone. The perfect relationship is the one you work at. Just like anything you learn, it takes openness, vulnerability and lots of practice.

Many couples have found ways to live together in some of the most challenging situations. For instance, we all need a restful sleep, but there are many people who can't sleep because of their partner's snoring. We know two women who love each other dearly. They cuddle in the mornings and afternoons, but sleep in separate bedrooms at night. We know another couple where each partner has her own private room for solace and space which helps them live more peacefully. Over time, experiencing much frustration and heartache, each couple has learned dance steps that allowed them to stay together.

Dianna: As a therapist, the metaphor of learning a new dance is very helpful in relieving stress in my clients. They imagine learning a new dance (salsa or hip-hop) and realize that it takes lots of dance lessons to get the steps right. When they apply that picture to the problems they're having, they relax a little bit and realize it takes much time, energy, openness, dedication and more knowledge to be successful.

Sheridan: We could have broken up many times throughout our almost 25 years together, but we continued to learn the dance steps. In learning the dance steps we learned about ourselves. My walls came tumbling down (walls I didn't even know I had), and Di learned to trust herself with me. Just imagine if we would have left our relationship. We wouldn't be able to look back at our journey together and see how we have both grown emotionally, and we wouldn't be able to experience our love continually deepening.

When your relationship gets hard and you want to call it quits, go back to your grounding place. That point in the beginning at which you liked your partner and then loved her/him. Sit down and talk honestly about what you want from your relationship and what you want in your life. Remember there are two of you! How you share space, your feelings, find balance and compromise are your dance steps. Practice them. You, too, can look back and be proud of your journey together. We are living proof.

November 2002

FAMILY — AT WHAT PRICE?

This is the time of year where families get together to eat, drink, and be merry. Are you gearing up and strategizing how you will be with your family? Will you tell them the truth about your sexual orientation and who you've been dating or living with? Or, is it best not to take your partner so they won't ask questions? Or, if you do take your partner, do you tell them she/he is your friend or roommate? If they ask if you're dating someone of the opposite sex, what will you say? This confusion occurs too much and too often and causes constant turmoil for many LGBT's. This stress is a huge price to pay for being our true selves. For you who are struggling today with the decision to be honest when facing your family, it's important that you be aware of the price you're paying when you stay in the closet and deny who you truly are. Think about all of the energy you exert by hiding, and the craziness you feel and the problems the closet causes in your relationships. There is the constant worrying if and when they will find out, as well as the negative tape of not feeling accepted by them. (Sheridan) Being accepted by my parents was important to me and still is but I had to learn to let go and live my life for me, not for them. My choices were to live a phony, unhappy life with them, or live real and happy life without them. My soul had died to the point of me denying my own needs. So with much soul-searching and hard work, I accepted myself. I owned me and became a free person. I no longer allowed my family's expectations to trap me. (Dianna) Sher was with me at all of my family gatherings. That's just the way it was. I accepted them—they accepted me. If they weren't going to accept me I wasn't going to accept them. No if's, and's or but's about it. I share this strength with my clients and friends. They must learn that they don't have to lose themselves in order to be accepted by others, especially their families. Family members are to love, care and support you and if they can't, why subject yourself to such hardship? Your parents don't own you or your rights forever. Parents are supposed to teach you to love and accept yourself. So, it's time you show your parents that you love and accept all of you. I believe it's a growing process that must occur within you so you will begin to value yourself and your worth. When you deny yourself, your soul dies; when you accept yourself, your soul lives. We know the ties between family are strong and these expectations are why so many LGBT's suffer so much for so long. We also know that too many have lost their lives as a result of this issue. They couldn't go on living with a dead soul. We have to stop this useless suffering and dying, literally and metaphorically. We have to stop, look, listen, and evaluate the price we're paying to maintain relations with our families. What's the worst that can happen, that they will reject you? So be it! At least this way you will have your self-respect and a soul that is alive and true. If you love and accept yourself, you will find your way with or without your family, because you matter. It can be done. You can be living proof.

Index

Acceptance, 2, 30, 45, 58, 109, 120
Adrenaline, 13, 28
Afghanistan, 2
America, xi, xii, xiv, 1, 2, 3, 11, 12, 13, 14, 15, 29, 30, 81,
Artichoke, 43
Asians, 1
Atheists, 13

Balance, 126, 127, 131
Barbara Boxer, 30
Bay Area, 30
Blacks, 1, 15, 29, 46, 114
Bondage, 41, 79–88,

Celebrities, 28
Chains, 15, 17, 41, 46, 79, 86
Civil Rights, 12,100
Comfort zone, 120–121
Commitment, 15, 30, 58, 79, 126
Communication, 79, 85, 121, 125–126

Denial, 58, 123
Discrimination, 1, 45
Diversity, 13,
Don't ask, Don't tell, xii, 1, 27
Dreams, 84, 86,

Emotional wounds 41, 42, 43, 48
Equality, 2, 13,

Family, 46, 47, 59, 85, 86, 103, 109, 110, 111, 117, 118, 119, 124–126, 128, 132
Fears, 2, 48, 59, 84, 112, 113, 114, 121, 128
Find Your Happiness, 87

Gay Pride, 29
Government, 1–3, 27, 28, 30, 58, 91

Harassment, 58,
Hatred, 47, 85
Healing, xiii, 41, 42, 43, 44, 46, 47, 48, 49, 58–62, 79, 82, 84, 85, 86, 114, 116, 117
Homophobia, 13, 17, 27, 28, 29, 41, 59, 85, 128
Honesty, xiv, 59, 71, 83, 87, 93, 118, 119–120, 125, 132
Human nature, 2

Immigrants, 15, 16
Injustice, 1, 31,
Inner Child, 81
Internalizing, x, 17, 27, 28, 29, 59, 85
Iraq, 2

Japanese, 29
Jews, 13, 29
Journaling, 87, 117, 137,

Kindness, 80

Language, 81, 85, 87
Latinos, 1, 29
Leadership, 15, 77

Mark Brigham, 30
Martin Luther King Jr., 11
Matthew Sheppard, 12
Media, 1, 28
Military, xii, 1, 2–3, 13, 27,
    111, 112
Music, 28, 61, 88, 117

Native Americans, 1, 29
Nature walks, 88

Oppression, 4, 18, 39, 101,
    114

Pacific Islanders, 1
Pain, 1, 2, 42, 43, 44, 45, 47,
    57, 77, 81, 82, 83, 84, 85,
    89, 111, 118, 123
Parents, 45, 70, 103, 110,
    117, 118, 119–120, 129,
    132
Peace, xvi, 2, 49, 86, 87, 115,
    116, 117, 118, 126
Pennsylvania, 30
President Bush, 91
Privilege, 3, 91

Race, 11, 15, 25, 110
Racism, 17, 48
Rejection, 37, 82, 86, 123,
    124
Relationship, 27, 30, 41, 44,
    45, 58, 81, 85, 110, 116,
    117, 118, 120, 123, 124,
    125, 129, 130, 131
Religion, 12, 30, 74, 91

Respect, xvi, 3, 15, 27, 58,
    68, 82, 83, 91, 120, 132–
    133
Rosa Parks, 15, 16

Sacrifice, 11, 12, 15, 19, 61,
    67, 83, 119, 128
Self-care, 129–130
Self-esteem, 44–45, 59, 79,
    81, 82, 116
Self-help tools, x, 59, 62, 79,
    87–98, 107, 117, 126
Self-worth, 15, 44, 45, 79,
    81, 82, 113
Sexual orientation, 12, 45,
    59, 71, 110, 111, 132
Society, 28, 30, 41, 46, 58,
    73, 81, 110
Soldiers, 13, 17
Soul-searching, 57–77, 86–
    87
Spirituality, 86
Support system, 85, 87

Teachers, 48, 59
Terrorist, xiv–xv, 1
True freedom, 30, 119, 120

Victims, 18,
Virginia Satir, 81

War, xii, 2, 11, 12, 13, 14,
    17, 27
We The People, 109
Whites, 12, 15, 28
World Trade Center, xii, 1,
    14

I'm Special Publications

YOU MADE IT!
WONDERFUL!
BUT YOU CAN'T STOP HERE!

YOU MUST CONTINUE FORWARD ON YOUR JOURNEY FIGHTING FOR YOUR FREEDOM AND THE FREEDOM FOR ALL PEOPLE.

REMEMBER TO ALWAYS
BELIEVE IN YOURSELF, AND
THAT BELIEF WILL CARRY YOU
WHERE YOU MUST GO.

I WISH YOU WELL
ON YOUR JOURNEY!

COOBODAY,

Dianna

About the Author

Dianna L. Grayer is a marriage and family therapist (M.F.T.) with her office located in the Northern California town of Petaluma. She counsels children, teens, adults, couples, and families—from all diverse backgrounds. In 1979 she earned her bachelor's degree from San Francisco State University, where she is in the sports hall of fame, and her master's degree from Sonoma State University in 1993. Over the past seventeen years, she has achieved or is still doing the following: foster parenting of 23 children; working as a group home counselor, a caseworker for a foster care agency, a facilitator of teen groups, a co-teacher of Fost/Adopt education classes, an instructor teaching Independent Living Skills (ILS) to teens getting ready to emancipate from the system, and a workshop presenter. She has published a self-help book, *Journaling: Getting to Know Yourself,* and is in the process of collaborating on a new book about ILS for those over eighteen years old. She has produced a communication game and a poster of her *I Have A Dream* poem, both launching in early 2003. Dianna has a children's book now being published, from which she has written a play; she hopes to cast it in the near future.

Dianna is multitalented. A woman with a vision. She is always creating self-help material to encourage and support those in need. She advocates for people to be true to themselves and believes as a result of honoring themselves they will live happy, productive and free lives.

When she isn't seeing a client or writing, Dianna is likely to be found playing basketball, remodeling, laughing, or playing cards or a board game.

If you found this book to be helpful in moving you forward in your life, and want to pass a copy on to a loved one or someone who would benefit from this book, you can order it below. Also check with your local bookstores and online sellers. If they don't have it, suggest that they do. Thanks in advance!

Order Form

Name_____

Address_____

City_____State_____Zip _____

Freedom Is Your Human Right!, ___copies, $16.95 each $_____

California residents please add applicable sales tax $_____

Postage and Shipping add $4.00 $_____

Total enclosed $_____

International shipping is extra, additional rates are needed. Please contact us for shipping rates to your location if outside the United States.

For more than 5 copies, please contact the publisher for quantity rates. Let the publisher pay for your shipping. Send your completed order form and check or money order to:

I'm Special Publications
P.O. Box 452
Petaluma, CA 94953

www.iamspecialpublications.com

Please autograph the book to

_____

Also available from the author is:

Journaling: Getting to Know Yourself $15.00 each

A writing book to move you on a personal journey toward becoming better acquainted and more connected to yourself.